Tarana Burke has always been struck by a commitment to justice and equity. As the founder of the 'me too.' movement and subsequent nonprofit, Burke works to dismantle the cycle of sexual violence and other systemic issues that disproportionately impact marginalized people. Burke's passion for community organizing began in the late 1980s and has spanned over three decades of working at the intersection of racial justice, arts and culture, anti-violence, and gender equity. She has received numerous accolades, including *Time* magazine's Person of the Year (2017), *Time's* 100 Most Influential People (2018), Sydney Peace Prize (2019), and *USA Today's* Women of the Decade in 2020. She is the coeditor of the instant *New York Times* bestseller *You Are Your Best Thing.*

'Searing. Powerful. Needed.' Oprah

'I will never stop thinking about this book.' Glennon Doyle

'Sometimes a single story can change the world. *Unbound* is one of those stories. Tarana's words are a testimony to liberation and love.' Brené Brown

'Burke sings a Black girl's song and *Unbound* stands alongside *I Know Why the Caged Bird Sings* and *The Color Purple*, as a coming of age story that is at once searingly painful, brilliant, and beautiful. Tarana Burke is known around the world for her activism and leadership. Now she will be known as an extraordinary writer.' Imani Perry, author of *Breathe*

'Burke's *Unbound* is one of those rare books that will unfold and welcome parts of us we thought we'd completely hid until the earth is gone. *Unbound* is the one we readers and writers have been waiting for.' Kiese Laymon, author of *Heavy*

'An unforgettable page-turner of a life story rendered with endless grace and grit.' *Kirkus Reviews*

'Intensely moving and unapologetically frank, Burke's fearless memoir will uplift and inspire the next generation of survivors, advocates, and truth-tellers.' *Publishers Weekly*

UNBOUND

TARANA BURKE

HEADLINE

First published in the UK in 2021 by
HEADLINE PUBLISHING GROUP

First published in paperback in the UK in 2022 by
HEADLINE PUBLISHING GROUP

1

Cataloguing in Publication Data is available from the British Library

ISBN 978 1 4722 9235 3

Offset in 10.8/15 pt FreightText Pro by Jouve (UK), Milton Keynes

Printed and bound in Great Britain by Clays Ltd, Elcograf S.p.A.

HEADLINE PUBLISHING GROUP
An Hachette UK Company
Carmelite House
50 Victoria Embankment
London
EC4Y 0DZ

www.headline.co.uk
www.hachette.co.uk

For Melinda, who never knew freedom.

For Kaia, so you always have freedom.

For Heaven, for helping me find freedom.

For Mommy, so that all you feel is freedom.

contents

prologue

The vibration of my phone nudged me awake. It was Sunday morning, and I was sleeping in. Through half-shut eyes I watched my phone slide across the nightstand. *Bzzzt! Bzzzt! Bzzzt! Bzzzt!*

I thought about the halfhearted promise I had made to my mom that I would try to go to church that morning. It had to be her pinging me with a reminder, and a slight pang of guilt kept me from looking at my phone. I figured not seeing the message was basically the same as not getting it at all, so I closed my eyes tighter and rolled over in bed. I needed the extra rest.

The night before I had been out late with my girlfriends. It was unseasonably warm for New York in the fall, and we had decided to go to our favorite local spot, Sexy Taco/ Dirty Cash. The bartender, Antonio, was a true mixologist, and ever since we came in one night and ordered what he deemed "wack drinks," he made it his personal mission to broaden our horizons. We never ordered off the menu when he was on shift. We simply sat at the bar and *got our life*— joyfully socializing the way Black women do—as he made us new concoctions. We'd ohh and ahh and giggle and flirt until we were feeling good enough to float on home. With my low threshold for liquor, that was usually two drinks.

That Saturday was no different. We sat around the bar trying new things, eating, laughing, and cutting up before we took the party out onto the streets of Harlem. By the time I got home and crashed, I knew full well that it would be a late sleep the next day.

About an hour after the first buzz, my phone vibrated again. This time it was a Facebook notification from a friend, so I opened my phone to look and she had tagged me in a post that read

This one rocks. Tarana Burke look. Me too. Predators are everywhere. Work, home, houses of worship, you name it.

_____

If all the women who I know who have been sexually assaulted or harassed wrote "me too" as a status . . . and all the women they know . . . we might give people a sense of the magnitude of the problem.

I grabbed the phone off of its charger in a panic and read the message again more carefully, thinking that the friend who posted it had written the entire thing. I was so confused about why she would do so without consulting me first. I'd been doing the work of bringing empathy into the fight against sexual violence for many years now using this language. I sent her a private message thanking her for tagging me and explaining that I had been working hard to relaunch my website and broaden the work around 'me too,' and that I didn't want to diminish it by creating a simple hashtag in response to the recent news stories. I had, of course, seen the media coverage of the Hollywood mogul who had been exposed—in not one but two bombshell stories—as a serial predator of women, confirming years of whispers and not-so-subtle innuendos from some of his famous collaborators. I had read the stories of the high-profile actresses who had courageously come forward to talk about the horrific things they suffered at this man's hands, and I had watched as the unfolding conversation reverberated across social media. Other than these women being survivors of sexual violence, none of what was happening in Hollywood felt related to the work I had been entrenched in within my own community for so many years. Seeing "me too," the phrase I had built my work and purpose around, used by people outside of that community, was jarring.

My friend was confused too. She explained that she hadn't created the original post or the hashtag; she was simply reposting it and giving me credit because she knew I had long been doing this work using that phrase. I asked if she minded deleting the post to slow down whatever was being spread. My heart dropped at the thought of inviting people to open up and share their experience with sexual violence online without a way to help them process it. I knew it could lead to emotional crisis in the absence of caring, empathetic environments. There was a knot growing in my stomach. This would be a disaster if it went viral.

"Maybe it won't catch on," I messaged as a rush of anxiety—and a creeping hangover—made my body flush.

And then she said it. "It's all over the internet."

My brain was scrambling. I went to my Facebook timeline and frantically scrolled up and down, but I didn't see a single post using #metoo except hers. I let my body relax a bit and then remembered to check my notification from earlier. It wasn't my mom guilting me about church; it was a text from another girlfriend with a screenshot of a series of tweets . . . all using #metoo. Underneath, she wrote, "Hey sis, this you?"

The blood drained from my head.

I sat up in bed and pulled out my laptop. It took less than thirty seconds on my Twitter feed to see the first #metoo tweet. I was not a prolific tweeter at the time and wasn't very familiar with how to navigate it. I quickly FaceTimed my nineteen-year-old child—my big-hearted, caring, gender nonconforming, free-spirited child and activist in their own right—who was deeply familiar with my work and had also set up permanent residence in the Twittersphere.

I didn't even wait for a hello. "Baby, have you seen people using #metoo online?" I asked, forgetting it was well before rise and shine for a Gen Y college student. They told me they hadn't, and I tried to explain that something was happening but that I couldn't quite find it.

"Search the hashtag, Ma," they groaned.

Annoyed, I asked for explicit instructions. They walked me through it, and with just a few clicks, hundreds of thousands of tweets flooded my screen. My life flashed before my eyes: all the work I'd done, all the things I'd been through. In a daze, I managed to say I'd call them back later before hanging up. I scrolled down and down and down, each hashtag feeling like a needle pricking my skin. Some of the tweets had pictures attached, some were full of emojis, and others used every last one of the allotted one hundred and eighty characters.

And they all said #metoo.

I slammed my laptop shut and tried to take deep breaths before the anxiety welling up in my chest took over. I got out of bed, walked into my living room, and opened a window. I let the cool breeze hit my skin, trying everything I could think of to calm down, but the quickening in my heart made it feel like I was doing a hundred-yard dash over hurdles. I picked up my cell and frantically dialed Vernetta, one of my best friend's, numbers. She didn't answer, so I called another one, Yaba. She answered. It turned out the two of them were together.

"Girl," I started, trying to steady my voice unsuccessfully before it all came spilling out, "someone turned 'me too' into a hashtag and it's all over the internet. I don't know what to do!"

Yaba is one of the most even-keeled and measured women I know. She doesn't excite easily and is not prone to histrionics. Hearing the distress in my voice, she knew exactly what to say.

"Just take a step back and breathe."

I listened to the calm of her voice as she reassured me that whatever was happening was not the end of the world and could likely be solved among our little group. My breathing steadied. The tears that had welled up in my eyes stayed pooled in the corners, and I tried to slowly collect myself.

"Now you said *what* is happening with 'me too'?"

I walked her through my morning and explained that I was watching the hashtag grow by the minute on Twitter. It was apparently on Facebook too, but not significantly in *our* community—meaning Black folks—on either platform. The tears I was fighting back started streaming down my face as I thought about how this had ballooned so quickly.

"This can't happen," I said through my tears. "Not like this! Y'all know if these white women start using this hashtag, and it gets popular, they will never believe that a Black woman in her forties from the Bronx has been building a movement for the *same* purposes, using those exact words, for years now. It will be over." I was now outright sobbing. "I will have worked all these years for nothing!"

Yaba put me on speakerphone so both she and Vernetta could try to soothe me and sort this out. My brain had switched gears, though. I was in full meltdown mode. Abruptly, I told them I had to go and hung up the phone. Yaba called me right back, and I sent her to voice mail, unable to catch my breath.

A text popped up on the screen. Bish, did you just send ME to VOICEMAIL?! I am going to give you a pass because you ain't in your right mind at the moment—but you got ONE time. Answer this damn phone! The note was so typical of her that it made me chuckle. I pulled it together enough to call back, and she once again put me on speakerphone before delivering some straight talk.

"Listen, you know *everybody* and *everybody* that knows you knows that 'me too' is yours. We've been watching you do the work for years. In this day and age, you gotta pull out receipts. So—pull out your receipts! Put them out there and let them know this already existed."

She was right. It had been a little over eleven years since I had been living and working in Selma, Alabama, and had started using the phrase "me too" as a way for survivors to connect with each other and to make a declaration to the world. I had gone all over the country—any and everywhere folks would allow me space—talking about how the exchange of empathy between survivors of sexual violence could be a tool to empower us toward healing and into action. I reassured myself that I had conducted enough workshops, participated in enough panels, and given out enough T-shirts and stickers to earn the right to say that this work, and the phrase that encapsulated it, was *mine*. And I did know a lot of people. My long and varied background in social justice work, arts and culture, and journalism had afforded me a collection of friends and associates across multiple fields who I knew would stand up for me if I asked.

I pulled myself together and went searching through my phone. I remembered a video my cousin took of me a few years earlier. I was giving a speech at the 2014 Philadelphia March to End Rape Culture explaining what the 'me too.' Movement was and why folks should join us in furthering the work. I was wearing a black miniskirt with pink stiletto heels and a pink and white striped blouse. Atop the blouse was a black tee that had the words ME TOO printed in bold, bright pink lettering. It was our signature T-shirt.

I watched the video again and took a deep breath. It felt like the "receipt" I needed. I drafted a message to go with the video and uploaded both to all my social media pages.

> It has been amazing watching all of the pushback against Harvey Weinstein and in support of his accusers over the last week. In particular, today I have watched women on social media disclose their stories using the hashtag #metoo. It made my heart swell to see women using this idea—one that we call "empowerment through empathy"—to not only show the world how widespread and pervasive sexual violence is, but also to let other survivors know they are not alone. The point of the work we've done over the last decade with the 'me too.' Movement is to let women, particularly young women of color, know that they are not alone—it's a movement. It's beyond a hashtag. It's the start of a larger conversation and a movement for radical community healing. Join us.

Once the message was out there, I reached out to my networks in every industry—bloggers, journalists, influencers, writers, activists, organizers, artists, filmmakers—and asked anyone who had any reach to repost or retweet or find some way to amplify my post.

And then I waited.

Without exaggeration, next to giving birth, this felt like the longest night of my life. I had an outpouring of support from friends and chosen family, all familiar with the work I'd been doing and how much of myself I'd put into it. Some were in the work with me—comrades in the fight to end sexual violence, particularly child sexual abuse. Others were organizers, nonprofit leaders, writers, and public figures. But despite the support, my fear lingered about everything I'd worked toward coming crashing down around me.

My post and video were being shared widely, and in my speech I had talked about how tired and scared I was that my work would be co-opted. That was how I felt watching this hashtag galvanize social media. I shared my anxieties in a group chat I had with several others who are in the work. I talked about how overwhelmed I was, how I needed time to craft a proper response and get my website and talking points together. I told them that I felt hopeless because I couldn't move at the speed of the internet. I had toyed with the idea of walking away from this work because it was so hard—and maybe this moment was a sign that I should give up. I had been trying in vain to amplify it for years, with zero resources and little support, and I was now going to have to fight a viral hashtag that probably wouldn't be connected to the origins of the work at all. I was dejected.

At this point I knew little of how the hashtag had started. I had no idea that the actress Alyssa Milano had sent out the first tweet. I didn't know the full extent of the responses, and I didn't know if my attempt to insert myself by posting an old speech was shifting the conversation at all.

I put down my phone and climbed back into bed, attempting to will myself to sleep. Maybe I could stave off the anxiety burning in my chest. I lay awake for a moment before giving in to the urge to flip open my laptop and search Twitter again. It had been a few hours since I checked on the status of the hashtag. Every time I checked there was a whole new wave, and I felt compelled to scroll through it all.

About an hour into my scrolling, I came across a tweet that just said #metoo with a link attached. The link led to the woman's personal blog where she had posted, in great detail, the story of her sexual assault in college. She wrote about how it wasn't until she saw all the #metoo posts that she felt she could tell the story publicly and be embraced and supported. She wrote of the shame she had been carrying for years, and how the burden of her trauma kept her from living a full life. She wrote that witnessing the sheer number of people boldly saying #metoo online had made her feel less alone. This complete stranger felt *less alone* by discovering how many others had been carrying secrets like hers. And she felt less alone by watching other strangers release those secrets into the world.

So many people had pulled these memories from the pits of their stomachs and the recesses of their minds. They came forward not knowing what would come next, but feeling far too compelled by the promise of community to let the moment pass them by. They hoped, for the first time, that they might feel less alone by sharing.

Here was a woman feeling less alone because she had found a place to be seen.

Her post landed on my spirit like life lessons often do: hard, fast, and with aching discomfort. I sat up in bed, tears flooding my eyes again. This time I cried for the anonymous woman. I cried for the sheer volume of tweets I had seen that day. I cried because, though I was exhausted, I knew exactly what was coming.

My lessons are never low-key and my assignment is always plain and clear once it is revealed. I am hardwired to respond to injustice. It doesn't always sit well with me, but I've learned the hard way not to ignore it. It's the same wiring that led to the creation of the 'me too.' Movement. It's what kept me working with children in the Deep South even when it required the kind of sacrifices that others might walk away from. And it's why I have always had a "community job" in addition to any actual paying job. From the moment I understood that organizing was the work that had to be done to respond to injustice, I knew I wanted to do it in service of my community. That realization—clear as a bell—came to me as a young teenager, and that bell rang again for me that night.

"What are you doing, Tarana?" I asked myself. I was overcome with a new emotion, and I could not have ignored it even if I had wanted to. In the Christian church, they call what I was grappling with *being convicted*. I knew better than to run from this or agonize about whose movement it was. God had shown up and checked me on that. I had spent the whole day wringing my hands and pulling my hair out trying to figure out how to save "my work." It took a story from a stranger for me to realize that my work was happening right in front of me. After deciding all those years ago that I wanted a life in service of community, in this moment I had to decide who I was going to be. Was I going to be who I said I was? The answer felt obvious. I didn't want to fight about who got what credit. I just wanted to show the world why a movement like this was necessary.

Back in 2005 when I started working on 'me too,' it was so difficult to get people on board—including those who claimed to be in the service of our community. Activists, organizers, youth workers, social justice warriors, and the like would agree that it was necessary work, and congratulated me for taking it on, but they still wouldn't do much to support or further our efforts. What motivated me to continue were the little Black and Brown girls who trusted us with their secrets, their pain, their shame, their worries, their anger, their fears, and their hopes.

It didn't take resources to introduce the possibility of healing into their lives. It didn't take wide-ranging support to stand up for them and others like them. It took vision. It took intention. It took tenacity. It took courage. And it took empathy.

I fell asleep with that on my mind and woke the next morning with a different fire. I didn't know who, if anyone, would listen, but it was clear that I had to share my vision for this movement with the world. It was clear that all the folks who were using the #metoo hashtag, and all the Hollywood actresses who came forward with their allegations, needed the same thing that the little Black girls in Selma, Alabama, needed—space to be seen and heard. They needed empathy and compassion and a path to healing. I wanted to be a part of making sure they had what they needed.

The journey that began that Sunday morning in the fall of 2017 is its own story—one you've likely heard, watched, or read about again and again. The story I'm going to tell is about how we got to those two simple yet infinitely powerful words: me too. The story of how empathy for others—without which the work of 'me too' doesn't exist— starts with empathy for that dark place of shame where we keep our stories, and where I kept mine.

The courage that trickled out of a young Black girl in the Bronx, and now from millions of others, formed the massive ocean that this movement has become. The essence of 'me too' is found deep in the marrow of this lifelong story. There is no *here* without where I was: stuck and scared and ashamed, a place I remained until the need to care for someone else's shame saved me too.

Every now and then, I find myself right back there with that scared little girl, but I can look to the road map this movement helped me chart to lead me home. I hope you are able to use my story of finding the courage to say "me too" to help you on your own path.

no alibi

Unkindness is a serial killer.

Death in the flesh sometimes seems like a less excruciating way to succumb than the slow and steady venom unleashed by mean-spirited, cruel words and actions that poison you over time. I guess that's why I can't stand the old children's rhyme: sticks and stones may break my bones but words will never hurt me. Every time I hear it, I think to myself: that's a lie. You can dodge a rock, but you can't unhear a word. You can't undo the intentional damage that some words have on your mind, body, and spirit.

Especially a word like *ugly*.

There is a funny way that some people interact with those they deem physically unattractive. Usually, they stare for about a half a beat too long. When they are noticed, they smile a small, guiltily fading smile. Then their eyes dart away and their posture falls into an unsettling mix of toddler and chimpanzee, as if they don't know where to move next. Suddenly, they are fascinated by the nothingness over your shoulder.

I know this act all too well and have seen it so often that I can spot it in the split second it takes to pass a stranger on the street. I can read the slight readjustments as discomfort churns through their body. There is just a millisecond of disgust, sometimes offset by embarrassment, and then—if confronted by my brief, unrelenting stare—guilt.

I know this because I'm ugly. At least that's what the world finds new ways to tell me every day.

As a very young girl, I thought I was just as cute as any other little Brown girl on my block. I was wrong. I remember when I first found that out. I was standing in line at the pharmacy, talking to this lovely father and his beautiful daughter. The little girl talked to me the whole time we were in line. Her father was engaged too. When they completed their purchase, the girl said goodbye and so did her dad.

They started to walk off and I moved up in line, but something made them stop within earshot. Perhaps he was counting his change or making sure he had everything before leaving. Whatever it was, I heard the little girl say, "Daddy, that girl looks like Amaya, right?"

Her father's tone, which had been so warm and friendly, was sharp and laced with hostility when he responded. It was a tone I would hear so many times over the next few decades. "No! She's too ugly to look like Amaya. You see how big her nose was? That girl is *ugg-ly*." And then he laughed.

The cut took time to register. *Was he talking about me?* I paid for my purchase and walked back home feeling numb and dazed. I was embarrassed.

Was I ugly?

When I got to my room, I pulled out a small photo album my mother had bought me and looked at the few pictures I had tucked away in the side flaps. There was one of me posing and smiling at the camera, like how I thought a model would. It was in a set of black-and-white pictures my mother's photographer friend snapped randomly one night. I studied and studied it. What did *ugly* even mean? No one had ever called me that before. I was tall and skinny and brown-skinned, with full lips and what my nana called a "bell pepper nose." I had been teased about each feature, but put together they had never equaled *ugly*. I didn't understand, and I wanted to. I *desperately* wanted to. But the man and his beautiful girl were gone. They had left me to figure it out on my own. I ran over every part of our interaction, from the moment I stepped in the line to the last words I heard from his mouth. I ran it over and over, and I came to the same conclusion every time: I just didn't know. But the word was lodged in the back of my mind, and it reared its head with every bit of evidence it collected.

In the pharmacy, I remembered wondering if the dad would think I was some kind of troublemaker. I had made small talk to show him that I was a good girl. I was extra polite. I was extra kind to his daughter. I was a *good* girl. But I was still *ugly* to him, and ugly is like a disease to some people. They act as if they might catch your ugly if you get too close. They stare with resentment, like it's your fault they have to see your face. It's like you are forcing them to share in the shame they imparted upon you in the first place.

This unkindness creates a particular kind of vulnerability. It makes the recipient ashamed, coercing us to be participants in our own torment. Somehow the world convinces us that its unkindness is the cost of admission for sharing space with the attractive—and we believe it. We don't just believe it, we welcome it, but in degrees. Not usually with a grin and wink—though sometimes we do—but mostly with a scowl, sometimes a foul word, sometimes an attitude, or even a few tears. But there is a small part of us that also feels alive and seen and grateful for that barely there acknowledgment. The flip side is being invisible, unseen, which is equally painful. And the thing is, either one will kill your spirit over time.

This new ugly "identity," this albatross around my neck, made me angry. Very angry. Like some weird version of Stockholm syndrome, I embraced my station in life as ugly. By high school, with a face full of acne and not enough money to be a Fly Girl, I created a new persona. I decided that if I wasn't to be beautiful or cute, then I would lean into what God left me with. I was smart and athletic and funny and outspoken. For those who insisted on reminding me of the burden I carried above my neck, I borrowed some of that unkindness, balled it up, and hurled it right back. I was mean. You could call me a name or try to make me the butt of your jokes—at your own risk. Most didn't try, and life was tolerable. Occasionally someone wouldn't notice I had *bacdafucup* etched across my forehead and rolled the dice.

It never ended well.

I was all too glad to unleash some of the fury I kept in the center of my chest. The truth of what I was, and the place I would always be relegated to, was my ever-present reality. It overwhelmed me. It was the thing I couldn't wish away, pray away, or fight away.

I once unleashed some of that fury on a guy on the subway. He got on the train with a rowdy bunch of friends, immediately drawing my attention. The way I was standing didn't allow for these dudes to see my face, but they could see my ass. As an athletic teenager who loved to dance, I had the kind of body Black boys my age apparently craved, and I had—all too many times—seen the disappointment, and experienced the danger, once I turned to face them. I had learned to travel in this body, with this face, in specific ways to ensure I made it to my destination safely. I tried not to wear form-fitting clothes, but my track body—medium frame, small waist, thick thighs, and large derriere—was hard to conceal. I immediately started looking for a seat where I could put my head down and hide.

I always tried to avoid eye contact and keep it moving, but that day I was slipping. Before I could slink into one of the small seats at the end of the train, I heard one guy say, "Damn, shorty thick!" My heart stopped. I knew what was coming next. I didn't have a hat on. My hair was pulled back from my face. I was on full display. As the dude approached me, with all of his friends watching, my heart started racing. I braced myself. The guy was about twenty feet away when I turned and gave him a full look. He stopped in his tracks and his face twisted into the *look* I had seen so many times before. He promptly spun on his heels and started walking back in the direction of his crew. I counted slowly in my head as one of them asked him what happened. Exactly seven seconds passed before I heard the thunderous laughter. I looked in their direction just in time to be throttled by the stares coming my way.

Before I could contain myself, I heard the words leaping out of my mouth. "Yo, what the FUCK are y'all staring at?!" I knew it was dumb. I was traveling alone, and the train was about to go underground, but I couldn't help it.

The dude who approached me got up and sneered. "You talking to me, bitch? I know you buggin'. You better keep that shit quiet, shorty."

But I couldn't. I never could. If I leave you alone, you should leave me alone. I thought I was doing everything right. I wasn't enticing him. I wasn't engaging him. I was standing quietly and minding my business. I knew my place. I was following the rules. Don't stir me up. Leave me alone. But he didn't, so I couldn't.

"Or else what?" I threw back at him, now staring directly in his face. I knew what I was risking, and it wasn't even the possible physical fight—I welcomed that more than the verbal jousting. I was nice with my hands, but I had only a small arsenal of comebacks.

"You got a lotta mouth for an ugly bitch."

And there it was. I instantly fell silent and stood frozen in my spot, as if standing perfectly still would somehow transport me through a portal into the twilight zone where ugly meant pretty and vice versa. But, as it had many, many times before, my stillness betrayed me. I had stepped out too far into the sunlight to suddenly wish for an eclipse to render me invisible. The crowd of guys that gathered behind him started oohing and cackling. The other passengers shifted uncomfortably, waiting for my retort.

It was just a moment before I shouted back, "Fuck you! You stupid bitch," but it seemed like it lasted an eternity, as if the milliseconds were conspiring against me. In that small window of time, I had begun breaking down inside. I was crying uncontrollably somewhere deep in my spirit. I was screaming *"Leave me alone!"* like a frightened child. I was begging for mercy. But all that could come out was nastiness to try and match his. He started a barrage of horrible insults, so I jumped up and hopped off the train as soon as we pulled into the next station.

I stayed on the platform for a while. I must have let at least three more trains pass by. I scolded myself for not being able to control my temper. I went over the incident again and again, wishing I had said and done things differently. I reimagined the whole scenario as it would have played out if he had thought I was cute.

And then I cried, knowing that the weight of this bitter, vitriolic unkindness and the all-consuming shame it brought was going to kill me eventually. It was a part of the death sentence I had received at seven years old in the moment I first realized I was alone. I used to pray to God, *Why me?*

But not anymore. I got my answer that day in the pharmacy when I was twelve with one word: I was *ugly*. Everything in my life after that validated what I believed was going to happen—and that I deserved it. Knowing when or how it would all end didn't matter, because this was a slow death and it was my cross to bear.

Alone.

me too

I n the winter after I turned seven years old, while playing outside with friends, one of the "big boys" in my small, close-knit neighborhood took me by the hand, walked me to a dark, secluded corner in our adjoined apartment buildings, and raped me.

He never let his tight grip loosen as he searched for an area where no one would see what he was doing. I was nervous because it was getting dark, and I knew I was too far away from where my mother said I should be—but I didn't utter a word.

My apartment building was connected to two other buildings. He first pulled me into the courtyard of one of the adjoining buildings and checked out the outside stairwell, but seemed to change his mind. My fear was growing as he continued to pull me farther down the block to the other building. Us little kids didn't venture into that building. It was partially abandoned, and its unlit areas were terrifying at night. He checked this outside stairwell and then quickly hurried me up the flight of stairs. I was quiet, mostly out of fear and confusion. Where was he taking me? And why?

When he told me to lie down on the cold stone steps, I complied. He leaned his body over mine while I laid there, stiff as a board and scared to death. He opened my coat and pulled my pants down past my knees, and then he opened my legs. He first penetrated me with his fingers and then tried to put his penis inside of me. I was frozen with fear. I remember the feeling of pressure against my small body. I remember him pushing and pushing. He finally stopped and stood up. He put his hand on his penis and began pulling on it before he ejaculated on me. I cried. I didn't know what *ejaculation* was, so for years I thought that he was peeing on me—like the way dogs peed on fire hydrants or random piles of garbage.

I had no real grasp of the gravity of what was happening, but I knew it wasn't right. It made me feel nasty and dirty and wrong, not realizing that *he* was wrong and that *he* was the culprit. I thought *we* were wrong.

He took my hand again and guided me back up the street toward my building, saying things to me that I can't remember. Over the years I have tried to fill in the blanks, both consciously and unconsciously. I imagined him saying, *this is what happens to ugly little girls.* I needed it to all make sense in my mind. It's unlikely he spoke those words. He probably said something that would have primed me to keep what was now *our* secret. Maybe he threatened me. Maybe he tried to bribe me.

The only clear memory I have is running through the litany of rules I had broken:

Never go off without permission.
Never be out of sight when you're playing outside.
Never come upstairs late.
Stay away from the grown-up boys.
Never ever let anyone touch your private parts.

What I knew for certain was that I was in big trouble. I hardly ever broke rules, and certainly never *this* many.

The boy walked me to my building and put me on the elevator. By the time I got upstairs it had grown dark outside, and my mother and stepfather were yelling out the window for me. I came into the house crying.

My stepdad, who was in the middle of calling me, turned around and bellowed, "WHAT HAPPENED?"

My mother started asking me what was wrong and what happened over and over.

I managed to stammer out, "A boy was bothering me . . . ," and in that moment I saw my stepfather's face change. It was a face I had seen before.

"WHO?" he yelled. "Who was bothering you?"

My stepdad, who I affectionately called Mr. Wes, was a six-four Caribbean man, born in Saint Croix and raised in

Harlem. He was twenty years my mom's senior, so when I was seven he was reaching fifty. He had a perpetual salt-and-pepper five o'clock shadow and a mustache with long sides that made his face feel scratchy when he gave me kisses. His voice was raspy, kind of like Harry Belafonte, but deeper, and he spoke loudly and with authority all the time. He wore a gold rope chain with his zodiac sign—Aquarius—and a gold pinky ring with a small diamond in the middle. He smoked his "smoke" and drank a fifth of Smirnoff every single day; he called it his medicine. Occasionally he would roll up a dollar bill when his friends gathered in the room with the door closed.

He was the sweetest, most loving gentle giant to me and the kids around the way, but he was scary when he was mad. I can recall him being mad at *me* only once in my life, but I had seen him mad at other people plenty of times. In our neighborhood—the block at 167th and Anderson just atop the now famous Highbridge steps—Mr. Wes and his group of friends loomed. There was Mr. Jimmie, who owned the bar downstairs from our apartment building; Mr. Kelly, who owned a bar in another neighborhood but stayed in ours; Mr. Rochelle, who worked for the post office and loved to gamble, and lose, according to my stepdad; Mr. Johnnie, Mr. Wes's "Puerto Rican brother," who was the happiest drunk in the crew and would often entertain us kids by playing his bongos in the alleyway; and Mr. Sam, who was the oldest. Like an informal commission, they watched over the neighborhood, and my stepfather was the leader. He was the neighborhood number runner, which was like a homegrown lottery in Black urban communities. Number runners were respected and essential community members, guaranteeing some occasional economic assistance. He operated out of a storefront where folks came to pick up the newspaper, play their numbers, shoot pool, gamble in the back, or hang out. He was the fun-loving, big-hearted guy who opened the pump so kids could get wet and cool off in the summer. He helped finance the annual block party and hosted bus rides with my mom to get families out of the neighborhood. He was also a cook in the army during the Korean War and would make mountains of food for the neighbors. Everyone knew if you were hungry, Mr. Wes would make sure you were fed. And if there was a problem in the neighborhood, before you called a cop, you called him.

Not too long before that night, I had seen Mr. Wes and his friends "take care" of a guy they had caught breaking into apartments. They paraded him down the alleyway that connected our three buildings and beat him—badly—in front of everyone who was crowded around. I was in the house as this was happening, but when my mom went to the window to watch, I was right up under her, peeking and trying to see what was going on. I watched as Mr. Wes and the others stripped the man down to his underwear and whaled on him, kicking and punching. When I made a sound and my mother realized I was watching, she quickly pulled me away, but it was too late. I saw it and would never forget it.

That was the memory that popped into my head when my stepdad demanded to know who had *messed* with me. I knew what would happen to that boy if I told—it would be worse than that man in the alley. And even more unsettling, I knew what could happen to Mr. Wes afterward. People in my neighborhood had gone away for less. So, at seven small years, I made a very adult decision to accept my fate and bury my secret.

I stammered a reply and stifled my tears. Mr. Wes eyed me skeptically, but I forced a smile and was excused. I didn't want to cause trouble for Mr. Wes, but I also didn't want to get in trouble. I began to put away the memory of what the boy had done to me because of what I thought it said about *me*. My insides strained to accommodate this new information, but they couldn't. And so they split. In the place I'd tucked away from Mr. Wes and my mom was the real me, the bad me. On the outside I would pretend I was good.

I did my best to mirror and mimic what "good girls" did, but occasionally I gave in to what I thought my "true self" was. In the first grade, at Sacred Heart Primary School, I kissed a boy at the water fountain. I let a boy catch me while playing catch and kiss at recess. I snuck off to lift my skirt outside the cafeteria when one of the boys asked. In my mind, I owed these things to anyone who found me out.

When I was molested again at nine, the split felt more like a shattering. It was another neighborhood boy, probably seven or eight years my senior. This time we were playing a game at the insistence of another girl. She seemed to like it, but I have no way of knowing whether that was true. *I hated it.* And because I hated it, the boy found it amusing to force me. He made us touch him and put our mouths on him and each other. He would take pictures with his Polaroid camera and then make us chase him through the house and eventually force us to do it all over again to get the picture back. It went on for years, the threat of the pictures always making us come back.

Then, the summer before I turned twelve, I cracked. I had a cast on my leg from corrective surgery to fix my pronated feet. It meant that I wasn't able to go away to camp like I usually did. He saw me outside on the block and asked me to come into his house for a minute so he could sign my cast. I knew what would happen, so I said I couldn't. But like always, he pulled out one of his Polaroids and waved it at me. I started to feel sick inside—having a cast and being unable to move freely made me more scared than usual. I made my way to his door where he stood holding it open. He marched me to his room, pushing me along. When we got there, he told me to lie down on his bed. I stood stiff as a statue, but he came over and shoved me on the bottom bunk. He laid on top of me and started rubbing me. He smelled like sweaty, clammy skin and festering bacteria. I started to feel nauseous and tried to find something else to focus on. It was becoming clearer by the minute what he intended to do.

Until now he had made me do things to him, then he would rub his clammy hands anywhere he wanted on my developing body, but this was different. I felt him fiddling with my belt and started praying. The belt had a metal fastener that you had to slide and click into place. It was my favorite type of belt because it came in all sorts of bright colors, but when it got old, the roller ball would stick. I don't remember the words I called out in prayer that day, but as I felt him struggle to loosen my belt, I knew God was answering my call. He yanked hard, causing him to stumble back and hit my cast. I screamed at the top of my lungs. I screamed the way I had always wanted to scream in that nasty, dark little room. I screamed for every moment he ever laid a hand on me. I screamed like I was jolted out of a nightmare. I screamed for seven-year-old me, who wouldn't dare scream.

He jumped on me, putting those disgusting hands over my mouth, but it was too late. I wasn't scared anymore. It's an eerie feeling when fear leaves your body. I was suddenly acutely aware of where I was and how much I didn't belong there. My fight-or-flight response converged as I struggled to get off the bed.

"GET OFF ME!" I screamed.

And then he just got up and started acting like I was crazy, asking me why I was bugging out. He yelled, "don't act like you don't like it now."

Confusion blended with anger as I got up and moved away from him. I picked up my crutches and started to hobble out of the room, but then, I saw his Polaroid camera hanging on the doorknob. I leaned on the doorknob like I was getting my bearings, and I took the camera. I don't know if he saw me, but he didn't chase me. I scurried through the doorway.

I had used the alley entrance at the back of the building to go into his house, but I chose to leave by the front. It was a shortcut, but it required me to go down a huge flight of stairs because the elevator wasn't working. I started down the steps slowly, almost sliding down, one at a time. I made it midway when my crutch slipped. I grabbed the railing to steady myself but dropped the camera. It fell all the way down to the bottom of the stairs, banging as it went. I stood still, watching it, my body rigid, until it came to a clanging stop. My heart was pounding as I again started the process of carefully making my way down, stair by stair.

I was focused on my feet, just about to reach the last step, when I collided with someone. I looked up to find our neighbor, Ms. Davis. She was an older lady who was a good friend of our family. I adored her and she adored me. She was so fabulous. She was always "sugar sharp," as the old folk would say. I had never seen her without a full face of makeup, complete with red lips; fancy, colorful earrings; and big, wide-frame sunglasses. She played her numbers in Mr. Wes's spot and always came to family and community functions. She would call me "my baby" with a big smile as soon as she laid eyes on me. To this day, I refer to so many little Black girls in the same way when I run into them on the street.

"Hey, my baby! Are you okay?" she asked, that big smile spreading across her face.

"I'm okay. I was cutting through the building to go home, but I almost fell down the steps." I tried to explain without sounding like something was wrong, but she was the kind of Black elder who listened to what your face and body told them more than the words coming out of your mouth.

"Oh, okay . . ." Her words were slow and skeptical. "So, whose camera is that?" she asked, pointing to the Polaroid lying broken on the ground. She looked at me with a little cock of her head. "It came flying down the stairs before you did."

"I found it," I lied.

"You found it? Okay. Where did you *find* it, then?" she asked, taking a half step back so she could take me in from head to toe. The look on her face told me the jig was about to be up. I hesitated for half a minute before I confessed.

"I took it from Draco's house, Ms. Morris's son—but he was bothering me!" It was like I was seven again and had said too much.

"Bothering you? Bothering you how?" She looked me directly in the eyes. And then she took her time taking me all in again. I didn't speak a word. My eyes were welling up as she put her hand on my arm, giving it a little push before she asked me again, this time in a lower, more deliberate tone. "Bothering you how?"

I had been in this moment before—when I had a chance to say something to my mom and Mr. Wes and didn't. I didn't know what telling meant because, again, I thought I would get in trouble too. I would have to answer for why I had been coming back to this boy's house time and time again. All the reasons sounded dumb in my head now. What if Ms. Davis didn't believe me? I wanted her to think highly of me. I didn't want her to know about the me I hid away. I wanted her to believe I was *good*.

My eyes started to water. Then, as if she could read my mind, she relented.

"Okay, calm down. I am not ya mama and daddy. I'm just going to ask you once—are you okay?"

I was full on crying.

"Yes, I'm okay now."

"Is this little camera thing going to cause you some trouble?" She stepped over to pick up the cracked camera.

"I don't know."

"Well, you don't have it now, then, do you? And you haven't even seen it, have you?"

I wasn't exactly sure what was happening, so I just shook my head vigorously in agreement because I suspected this was a good thing.

"Okay then, so you're fine, right, my baby?" she said, smile returning.

"Yes, I'm fine. Thank you, Ms. Davis," I replied politely, wiping my tears away.

She helped me down the last few steps to the landing and turned to go. Right before she left, she called out to me.

"These little boys can't keep their damn hands to themselves, my baby. You got a daddy who will go to his grave to protect you, so be careful, because we need Big Wes around here."

"Okay," I said quietly as she disappeared up the stairs.

Those few minutes I stood there with her were the closest I had ever come to feeling seen in my short life. I thought she knew what happened, but I couldn't be sure until she spoke those last words. I am positive she meant well. She didn't know that I had already opted to carry this burden when I was just seven years old to protect my beloved Mr. Wes from the ruin that I imagined him being locked away would bring to my family. She couldn't have known that when she introduced this unspoken vow of silence between us, the burial ground I had made inside myself for all my secrets was beginning to fill up. She didn't know I was desperate for a lifeline. So I took her advice, and I found space for this secret in that vast cemetery I carried in my soul.

I always wonder why they knew I wouldn't tell. What was it about me? What did they know? Did they see through my "good girl" charade? I have filled in the blanks with my own insecurities and post-traumatic ideations for years, but I can't say for sure. As good as I wanted to be, it was evident—in my small child's mind, at least—that I wasn't innocent in practice.

I started to settle into a new reality of who I *really* was—not the sweet, smart girl that my mom and family saw me as, but as this gross, fast, ugly girl with dark secrets. Before I reached puberty, I learned two things: how to smile and perform the role of good girl and how to hide the nasty, dirty, fast girl I thought I really was. At the time, not much felt authentic in my life except my love for my family and my love for learning.

I was a grown woman before I truly understood the word *rape* and was able to relate it to my experience. Language like *rape*, *molestation*, and *abuse* were foreign to me as a child. I had no definitions and no context. Nobody around me talked like that. I may have heard adults say things like, "you know he likes to 'mess with' little girls" or "you know you can't trust him around no kids," but no one had truly explained it to me. No one said things like, "You know so-and-so got caught raping a girl." The older women in my life—whether it was my mother or my aunt or the women in my building, who looked at me as their sweet baby—taught me plenty about protecting myself and my private parts. *Never let anyone touch your private parts*, they'd say. But I wasn't told *why* I had to protect my private parts, just that it was imperative *that* I did. Because of this, when I thought of my experience, I didn't hold my abusers accountable—I held myself to blame. In my mind, they didn't abuse me. I broke the rules. I was the one who did something wrong. It was this thinking that also kept me from ever identifying as a survivor. I didn't even identify as a victim.

I remember conversations in high school where girls teased me about being a virgin. As they laughed at me, I would think, *if only they knew I lost my virginity at seven.* That's what I believed. And as painful as that shame was, I also believed that I deserved the pain. I deserved to be tormented by flashbacks and anxiety and fear. I deserved whatever agony awaited me, because I broke the rules. I carried that. I carried that pain, heavy on my back and deep in my flesh. The weight sat on my shoulders, every day, slowly crushing me.

uptown baby

I am a third-generation Bronxite and was born and raised in New York there in the early '70s. My grandfather, Joseph Burke, was one of the first Black babies born in Lincoln Hospital in the late 1920s. His mother, Martha, came to the United States through Ellis Island from the island country of Saint Kitts in 1922. Grandaddy met my grandma, Willie Mae—who was raised in South Carolina and relocated when she was seven—on Lyman Place in what is known as the Banana Kelly section of the Bronx. He had stepped in to break up a fight between my grandma and her then-boyfriend,

Pete, who thought he could put his hands on her and get away with it.

As the story goes, my granddaddy stopped my grandma from going upside Pete's head after he raised his hand to hit her. She had grabbed a broom from the storefront they were standing near and started whaling on Pete. My granddaddy pulled her off Pete, then insisted on walking her home to comfort her. Somewhere between the brouhaha and her front stoop, Granddaddy decided, very definitively, as he often did, that she was "the one." He told her that he had been drafted to go to war—World War II—but that he would come back for her. Grandma says she paid him no mind and "went about her business" when he left.

While in the armed services, my granddaddy was in an airplane accident that nearly killed him, and he was sent home after serving just eighteen months. Once discharged, he kept his word to my grandma and showed up at my great-granddaddy's door asking to court her. She told her father that she didn't know who the heck he was. She did, of course, but she wanted to see how serious he was. He came back three times before she agreed to go on a date. She went out with him that day and a few days after that—and then, as he would often say, she became his last girlfriend.

My grandparents made a good life in the Bronx. Grandma was a nurse and Granddaddy worked for General Motors, which might have placed them in the upper middle class instead of working class if they hadn't had six children—my mother was the oldest. My granddaddy was the patriarch and head of household. He was strong willed and dominant. His word was law and his views were gospel. His golden rule was family first. Burkes mattered before anyone else. He and my grandma raised their children to be self-aware and smart, like them. He was a self-taught scholar of Black history and gourmet chef. He believed in the teachings of the Honorable Marcus Mosiah Garvey and Malcolm X, among others, and if you were in his presence for any extended period of time, you knew it.

We were what some would call a pro-Black family. My granddaddy believed in celebrating Blackness in as many ways as possible. Once my younger cousin, who was born the day after Malcolm X's birthday, said that he didn't know who the venerated Black leader was. My granddaddy went out on the spot and bought a birthday cake to celebrate Malcolm X. He used the celebration to teach my cousin about our own Black shining prince.

My mom, heavily influenced by my granddaddy, was engaged in the Black liberation struggles of the '70s and put me in an Afrocentric daycare, where I was learning Swahili and African dance at just three. Grandaddy believed in telling the truth about America and who we were in relation to it. I wasn't allowed to do things like wear red, white, and blue or participate in the Pledge of Allegiance. "What are you pledging to?" he would say. "This country doesn't keep its promises!"

As it often does, the patriarchy ran deep in our beloved patriarch. When my mom got pregnant during her junior year of college, family folklore says that my granddaddy was so angry he refused to speak to her for months. There was no evidence of that anger after my birth, though. I was the apple of his eye. My biological father was never a part of my life. I have never met him and have only limited information about him. My mother was my primary caretaker, but my granddaddy was larger than life for me from the first time he picked me up. Growing up the oldest of six kids in the '50s and '60s more than prepared my mother for raising a child of her own—even in an often-unforgiving city like New York. But the Bronx was a different animal.

What most of the world knows about the Bronx comes from the images of burned-out buildings and poverty-stricken Black and Latinx youth that littered the newspapers and voyeuristic art exhibits of the '70s and '80s. "The Bronx is burning" was a popular way to talk about my hometown then because of the rash of arsons that took away more than half of the livable properties in some census tracts. My borough has always been more than that, though, and for me it's almost like another family member. It was the rich cultural and political landscape of the borough that made such an impact on how my mother raised me—entrenched in the Black Power ethos of the moment. It is true that there were very few resources in the hood, but it was the first place I learned the value of using what you have to create what you need. People struggled, but they also built. The stories of neighborhoods reclaiming and rebuilding burned-out buildings don't often get told. But when I think of my own journey to healing, so much of it mirrors the power, resilience, and tenacity of my family and my borough.

Looking back now, I wish these things had been enough to protect me and others like me from the evils hidden deep in its city blocks, but they were not. There was always some new challenge or trauma, something lurking around the corner waiting to haunt me. Mr. Wes, who'd come into our lives as such a bright spot, was taken away, just like everything else.

Mr. Wes had been with my mother for almost a decade, and he was a beloved extension of the Burke family dynamic. He had four children besides me. Two biological, Roxanne and Ramona, and two other stepchildren from previous relationships: Kevin, who was smart and funny and charming but rarely came around, and Anthony. Ant, as most people called him, had been in and out of prison since I was little and was no stranger to the streets. He was fun and tough and would let me hang off his big, muscular arms when he worked out. I was also his mini caller ID long before the technology came about. With his caramel brown skin, bulking muscles, and unmistakable uptown swag, he always had ladies calling him. I would answer the phone and say their name out loud. "Hi, Diane, nice to meet you. I'm Tarana, how can I help you?" He would either take the phone and say, "That's my little sister," or he'd shake his head no, and I would say he wasn't home and hang up.

He never stuck around for long, but it was always better when he was there. My mom and Mr. Wes had parted ways—or something like that—and we had moved out of Mr. Wes's house and into our own place across town. I was still over at Mr. Wes's house almost daily because I went to school around the corner. I even went there on some weekends to hang out with my friends. On one particular Saturday night, when I was in the seventh grade, I was home with my mother. I was washing up before bed when she came into the bathroom looking like she was going to be sick.

"Anthony got shot." The words landed on me while I stood in my nightgown, brushing my teeth over the sink. I don't know why—maybe because I was a kid, or because I had never experienced a death, or because I was shocked by her sudden, abrupt delivery—I burst out laughing.

"*Tarana*," my mother said sharply. "Anthony is dead."

I stopped laughing.

Apparently, one of the women Anthony was seeing had a long-term boyfriend who had come home from prison and found out about their relationship. The boyfriend and his people trooped from Brooklyn to the Bronx and showed up to a party where Anthony was supposed to meet the girl. A shoot-out ensued.

Someone ran around the corner to get Mr. Wes. He'd shown up, pistol blazing, and found Anthony shot but alive. Anthony, who was a knife guy, had managed to stab and critically wound the boyfriend. What happened next was hazy and patched together from firsthand accounts and court documents. Mr. Wes turned to answer a shot, not realizing Anthony was right behind him, and shot Anthony in the back of the head.

For years, I carried so much guilt for laughing when my mother told me, but the guilt that stuck with me the most was the guilt for why I cried. I loved Ant, but my tears were more for Mr. Wes than my stepbrother. Mr. Wes was arrested and put on trial, and suddenly, everything that year felt held together by scotch tape and a prayer. Mr. Wes's oldest daughter, Roxanne, and her boyfriend, Mike, moved into his apartment. I hadn't seen them around much before; they were what grown folks called "out there." Roxanne was an early adopter of crack, the latest drug craze. Both she and Mike ran the streets and struggled with drug dependency. I no longer enjoyed going over to Mr. Wes's place—he was locked up and they'd trashed the apartment. I only went by to find out if there was any news from the trial.

The day the verdict came down, I was walking into Mr. Wes's building after school as Mike was coming out. We barely ever spoke, and I was prepared to walk past him, but he stopped me in the courtyard.

"Trial is done," he said, lighting a cigarette. "They got him. Wes is gone!"

I just stood there.

"What do you mean?" I asked, knowing exactly what he meant.

He took a pull on his nasty cigarette and continued. "They got him. He outta here!" he repeated, this time with a little chuckle. "Fucked up shit."

Then he walked away, leaving me stunned and struggling to understand what had happened.

There was something about the way he said it all so casually. He didn't seem to care about Mr. Wes, and that made me want to fight him right on the spot. But I knew my age and size meant nothing to him. If I swung, he would swing back.

I walked into the building and made it as far as the elevator vestibule before I broke down. I slumped to the floor in my school uniform, crying dramatically the way my mom frowned upon. I threw my book bag, and all the papers fell out and scattered across the lobby. I crawled around picking them up, still crying and crying.

I never went upstairs. I gathered myself and left the building to head home.

It felt like everything had converged on me all at once. In everything I had endured already, Mr. Wes was one of the brightest spots. I'd never used his protection, but I knew it was there for me, and that was something. I hadn't wanted to taint his view of me as a good girl by needing it. I wanted him to keep loving the version of me he was so happy to see and proud to brag about. I didn't want him to know anything about the girl I saw when I looked in the mirror. I had to preserve the good for him, and for my mommy and granddaddy and my uncles and aunt.

What was I supposed to do without Mr. Wes?

The thing I had sacrificed my soul to prevent happened anyway. Mr. Wes went to jail. Not for killing one of my abusers but for accidentally killing my stepbrother. It still felt like I was the one who had messed everything up. I wasn't sure how, but I believed that this, like every other bad thing that had happened to me, was somehow my fault.

acts of contrition

Being Catholic—particularly, being a confused little Black girl and a survivor who was Catholic—simultaneously saved my life and, in retrospect, threw it further into turmoil. We were not a Catholic family by tradition. My grandfather, who was West Indian and raised Catholic like many of his *bredrin*, stepped away from the church after being mistreated in a Catholic boy's home in the '30s. As a result, he had a scathing view of Catholicism and didn't raise his six kids in the church. But he didn't bar them from joining either. Instead, he allowed them to choose their own religious or spiritual practice when they were old enough to understand what they were getting into.

My mother, the eldest of the six, decided to become Catholic when she was twelve. At the time, the family lived across from Saint Athanasius Church. It is a legendary church that has served the people of the South Bronx, particularly in the Banana Kelly area, for over a hundred years. It was a cornerstone of the community. Catholic churches in New York are like Baptist churches in the South. They seem to be everywhere, especially in low-income and immigrant communities. The Bronx, which ranks fourth in size and last in wealth out of the five New York boroughs, has the second-largest number of Catholic churches (behind Manhattan).

My mom decided to join the church because of the weekends she would sit on her stoop and watch the festivities, weddings, and baptisms across the street. She said that people always seemed so happy. She also had memories of being treated well and taken care of at an after-school program at Casita Maria, a community center run by the nuns of Saint Athanasius. It makes me wonder what she needed shelter from at that age.

She was a bit of a late starter in the religion, so she signed up for sacrament classes, was baptized, and made her first communion all within the same month. That was May 1963. The following year, after she turned thirteen, she completed the last of the three-step process with the sacrament of confirmation and officially became a member of the Catholic Church. By the time I came along about a decade later, she had long stopped attending church regularly.

She'd given it up around the time she finished high school four years earlier. Still, she had me baptized when I was an infant, and at six years old, I started first grade at Sacred Heart Primary School in the Bronx. It had less to do with her being Catholic, though, and more to do with her being a working-class single mother trying to give her child the best possible advantage in life.

I didn't enter the school as a practicing Catholic, but I took to the teachings rather well. The rules were simple: read the Bible, spread the "good news," be kind and generous to others, pray, and confess. We wore burgundy, white, and gray–plaid uniforms with crisp white button-up shirts and small crisscross ties. We had a routine for everything from going to the bathroom to playing at recess, and if we ever had a doubt about whether we were good, bad, right, or wrong, the ever-present sisters and the brothers would remind us. The little girl who was desperate to show the world that she was *good* needed this regimen. According to those rules, although I had defied God by being sinful, God would forgive me. God wouldn't forget my sins, but that was okay as long as I was still allowed in his sight. He was *merciful*.

Going to mass, praying the rosary, and reading and sharing the "good news" were a lifeline to me as I worked my way back from the unspeakable sins I felt I'd committed. It was a complicated, tangled web in my head. I would go to confession regularly to confess a "cover sin"—lying, swearing, or something else instead of what I really held inside. I'd quietly ask God for forgiveness for lying, and then I'd redeem myself by doubling whatever penance the priest gave for the cover sin. He would instruct me to pray my rosary, starting with the Apostles' Creed, and to follow that with some number of Hail Marys and Our Fathers. In my mind, if I just doubled that number, I would set things right.

I loved confession. It was my favorite part of being Catholic besides communion, and I took it very seriously. We made confessions during school hours, so I didn't have to worry about being embarrassed to go into the box. It was just part of our schedule. Every student had to do it no matter what. When I came out of the confessional, I would immediately go to a pew to get started on my rosary and pray vigorously, but not publicly. I prayed my first round like everyone else, all the while promising God to finish before the day was out. To pull off my good-girl sham, the other students couldn't think that I had more to confess than they did and therefore more assigned prayers. I finished my prayers while in the lunch line, at recess, or during a bathroom break. As long as I got through it in my head, I had made good on my penance.

When all of the students had finished confessing and were waiting in the pews, Father O'Donald would come out and lead us in the Act of Contrition prayer.

"Oh my God, I am sorry for my sins. In choosing to do wrong and failing to do good, I have sinned against You and your Church . . ."

In that moment, saying those lines, I felt honest. It was the only time I allowed myself to peek out from behind the veil that separated me from the other girls, the *real* good girls. I felt bad for pretending to my classmates, like I was lying. Telling the truth even for one moment was a relief.

I was carrying so much shame—more than any child should have to confront. But like pain and suffering, shame has no age requirement. There is no set cutoff or start. It's just there one day and doesn't leave. At least not of its own free will. On my luckiest days the shame sat on my spirit like a thin film of dust. I saw and felt it, but it wasn't enough to disrupt things. On the worst days, it was like sliding down a muddy slope, helplessly sinking into the trap below.

On one of these bad days I was supposed to be in the kitchen doing the dishes. I was standing at the sink, washing out cups the way I was taught: a little dish detergent on the rag, use the rag to soap the inside of the cup, and then clean the outside and the rim with the rag before rinsing it thoroughly and placing it in the dish dryer.

I finished the last cup and started rinsing the soap out of the rag, but the water got cold. I rang the dishrag out several times to make sure the soap was out, but more small white bubbles kept appearing. As I rinsed it in cold water for the third or fourth time, I started to think about the taste of the soap. I dared myself to try it. Tilting my head down, I held up the rag to let a drop of the cool, soapy water drip in my mouth. Then I heard my mother's voice from the kitchen door.

"TARANA. JANEEN," she roared.

She always said my first and middle name when she was pissed at me.

"What the hell are you doing? Are you crazy?"

She flew into a rage, screaming at me. Busted, I could only stammer out a very guilty, "Nothing!" I was confused by my own actions. She was probably just grossed out, but her yelling made it seem like this was a way more serious infraction.

"I have never in all of my life seen something so nasty and stupid!" She kept screaming. "Do you KNOW what I use that dishrag for, *Tarana Janeen*? Huh? Do you KNOW? I scrub the GOOK off of the bottom of the dirty, burnt pots! I killed a damn baby ROACH with that rag and washed the body down the sink. That's the dirty, nasty thing you put in your mouth, little girl!"

As she yelled, I stood staring at her, wondering in my own small head why I had done something so gross.

"Is that what you are? A dirty, nasty, used-up dishrag?" she seethed.

Hot tears fell down my cheeks, quick and messy.

"Huh?" she demanded.

"No," I stammered sheepishly.

Her tone eased just a bit, like she realized this was an outsized reaction. "Go in the bathroom and wash your face and brush your teeth and your *tongue*!"

I'm sure my mother thought I was crying because her yelling upset me, and it did. My mother didn't curse much, almost never in fact, but she could reduce a grown man to tears without profanity when she was mad. It didn't take much for her to go from zero to furious. But it wasn't the yelling alone that made the tears fall. It was confirmation of what I thought I truly was—dirty, nasty, and used up.

While I was still attending Sacred Heart, my mother became serious with the man with whom she eventually had my little brother. Mr. Eddie had been around for years. He was from the neighborhood, so I had seen him a lot while growing up.

In fact, my friends and I were in awe of him as little kids because he could skate backward up the hill while listening to music. Mr. Eddie was very different from Mr. Wes. He wasn't interested in being a father figure to me. He made jokes about Mr. Wes being in jail. He made jokes about my mother. He spoke recklessly about my family. He was mean and rude and brash for no reason, and the opposite of everything I knew and loved about Mr. Wes. He barely talked to me except to bark orders with such disdain that it felt like he despised me. I barely even knew him, so I didn't understand why.

His introduction into our lives marked a sharp turn in my relationship with my mother. Before Mr. Eddie, she was the only one who disciplined me, outside of maybe my grandparents. I got in trouble with any number of adults, but it was always my mom who did the actual disciplining. She would become livid if a nonfamily member ever touched me. She once marched into my school and physically threatened my teacher for using a ruler on me in class. I once saw her grab a butcher knife and run outside to confront a white boy who slapped me in the park. Until Mr. Eddie came into the picture, my mom had zero tolerance for anyone who thought they had authority to discipline me—or, God forbid, lay hands on me. But then he came.

My mother had raised me to be inquisitive. We were close, like single mothers and daughters often are. I read a lot and was inquisitive, which made me conversant with adults in a way that a lot of my peers were not. All of that went against how Mr. Eddie believed children should behave. My talking irritated him, and I talked a lot. It got on my mother's nerves occasionally too, but never once did she tell me to shut up in a mean way. In fact, it was almost a forbidden phrase in our house. She may have snapped at me to be quiet when I was especially chatty, but never did she have the kind of rancor and disdain that Mr. Eddie spewed my way.

It wasn't long before I realized just how different things were with Mr. Eddie. I don't even remember what I was talking about the night it dawned on me. Perhaps it was something on television. I was going on and on to my mother, talking and laughing with her. Out of nowhere, Mr. Eddie jumped up out of the bed and shouted, "Shut the fuck up! Damn. You've been talking for over an hour! Children should be seen and not heard. Damn!"

My head swung around in disbelief as I looked at this man. He had barely even talked to me up until this point, and now he was cursing at me. I turned back to my mother, waiting for her to drop the hammer. My mother, the woman who once told a man who slapped me in the face at the supermarket for bumping into his cart, *"I don't care if she called you a barrel full of motherfuckers. You put your hands on my child and now you have to die"*—right before punching him so hard that she broke his jaw. My mother, who was the straightest shooter and the toughest person I knew.

Instead, she looked at me with a pitiful expression and said, "Just go in the other room, Tarana."

That's it. And I, wide-eyed and stunned, got up and looked around like Dorothy, trying to identify this new, strange land I had entered. I didn't cry. I left in a daze and sat waiting in the other room. I listened for my mother's roll of thunder to hear my cry and correct this injustice. I waited for her to do what she had done so many times before, what she was known for. "*You touch this one and you got a death wish*," she always said, pointing at me. "*I don't play about me and mine*," she'd promised over and over. That is who, and what, I knew to be true. But as I sat there, it became very clear that those truths had shifted.

His nasty behavior only got worse. I never got to hear what he told my mom, if anything, after one of his violent outbursts, but what I told her never seemed to be enough.

When my brother was born about a year after the cursing incident, I was sure that Mr. Eddie would never leave. Except he did. He left and came back more times than I can count, and each time it felt like my mother would get meaner and more distant, further from the woman I knew. I used to be her sidekick. She would dress us alike, buying sweatshirts and ironing on matching letters and patches. When she was with Mr. Wes, we would go out as a family. We would pile into his brown, 1980-something Nova and drive to Beefsteak Charlie's on Fordham Road or to the steakhouse down on Thirty-Fourth Street. We would be eating and laughing and having a good time when Mr. Wes would suddenly whisper loudly, "*Here, put this in your purse!*" He was always trying to take anything that wasn't nailed down, and mommy would chastise him. "*WESLEY! Put that back! I am* not *putting that in my purse!*" I would be in a fit of giggles, and eventually my mother's annoyance would cede to Mr. Wes's fake innocence. "*What?*" he'd ask in his growly voice with a hint of Saint Croix spilling over the Harlem intonation. "*I'm just a poor man tryna make it in the world . . .*" and we would all start laughing.

She didn't laugh like that around Mr. Eddie. It was like he had a spell over her. Nobody made my mother do anything she didn't want to do. She said what she wanted and moved how she wanted and lived the life she wanted. She could defend herself in any situation and could defend me from any harm that she saw. So why didn't she see this as harm? Why didn't she defend me? All I saw was her choosing this man's love over our happiness, and it tore me up inside. I didn't understand that on the inside maybe my mom was still that little girl sitting on her steps, watching the happy faces going in and out of church, longing for what she saw as joy and love. I didn't understand for far longer than I should have.

breathe again

My life had shifted because of my mother's relationship, and as I struggled more at home, I leaned into the church. Shortly before I had my own sacrament of confirmation into the Catholic Church, my granddaddy decided he needed to intervene in my love affair with Catholicism. One day, after seeing that I had finished reading my mother's copy of *Roots* by Alex Haley, he decided that I was ready for some "better history," as he called it.

He took me for a ride down to Harlem to one of his favorite spots, Liberation Bookstore on Lenox Avenue, and bought me two books: *They Came before Columbus* by Ivan Van Sertima and *Before the Mayflower* by Lerone Bennett Jr. He told me he had nothing against the Bible or Christians, but a lot of our folks, like the ones in *Roots*, stayed in chains long after they were taken off because their minds were chained to the Bible I loved. If I was going to read the Bible, he said, I needed to read these historical texts alongside it.

My mother had raised me as a bookworm, and so I spent most of the eighth grade doing exactly what my granddaddy had said to do. As fast as I could read a book, he'd recommended a new one. I started caring less and less about confession and started asking Father O'Donald harder questions during his weekly visits to our classroom.

Is it true that Catholics were slave traders and didn't do anything to help enslaved Africans until it was too late? I remember asking him once. He glared at me over his small wire-framed glasses as he stumbled through an answer about how the Catholic Church evolved over time. In turn, I stared back defiantly at the pulsating vein over his eyebrow. I had found a new thing to become: radical.

Fall of '87 was my freshman year of high school, and I was starting at Harry S. Truman. In 1987 in the Bronx, the only thing to be was a 'round the way girl. LL Cool J would really run it down for us a few years later, but if you were young, Black or Brown, and alive, you already knew what time it was. Hip-hop was our way of life. Our clothes, music, hairstyles, attitude, and aspirations all flowed from what people called the "soundtrack to the streets." I loved every bit of it.

I was desperately trying to separate myself from the eight years I had spent in Catholic school—years the new radical me now thought of as brainwashing. My mom couldn't understand why I wanted to go to the public school instead of continuing on at the Catholic high school, but public school was free, and I suspect she let me have my way because it also unburdened her financially.

Truman had a decent academic reputation, which helped to settle my mom, but it also had a legendary reputation for violence—that unsettled me. There were all kinds of stories of girls getting jumped and slashed or stuck up after school. On all sides but the front, the school was surrounded by Co-op City, a residential community made up of about thirty-five high-rise buildings with nearly fifty thousand residents about thirty minutes north of Bronxdale Houses where I lived. Co-op was a city of its own. It was a bastion of working and middle-class, mostly Black folks, but it functioned like many of the public housing complexes in the city—insular and identity driven. People from Co-op always let you know they were from Co-op, and not just from the complex but the specific section, the most notorious being Section Five. The front of the school faced the stretch of I-95 that made up the New England Thruway, and across the highway was a part of the Bronx dubbed "the twos" or "the two hundreds" because the street numbers ran into the two hundreds. Somehow, over the years a feud of sorts had developed between Co-op and the two hundreds, which was heavily populated by Caribbean folks. If you attended Truman and were not from one of these two areas, your allegiance was quickly determined by who you chose to run with. The rules weren't hard and fast, but they were clear enough to make students from the outside tread lightly.

I was an outsider—in more ways than just geographically. There was no harassment for being smart. Everyone was pretty cool about it as long as it was clear who you were. If you were a smart kid, you hung with other smart kids and did "smart kid things" like joining the honor bowl league or science club. If you were a tough kid, you clapped back at teachers and challenged everyone who got in your crosshairs to a fight. If you were a cool kid, you wore all the latest fashions and did I don't know what, because I wasn't one of them at Truman.

I landed in an undefined area. My mom initially required that I wear only skirts—long skirts—to school. She wanted to continue the modesty and uniformity of Catholic school. The only other girls who wore skirts all the time were either deeply religious, like Seventh Day Adventists or Jehovah's Witnesses, or they had "knowledge of self," meaning they had allegiance with the Five Percent Nation—a younger, slightly more authoritarian offshoot of the Nation of Islam. I was none of the above, but because I dressed the part I got lumped into at least one of these categories on a daily basis. Few things were as nerve-racking in late '80s New York as being approached by a group of dudes who were calling you "Earth" and talking about the "mathematics" for the day. I stood out like crazy in a sea of girls drawing style inspiration from rappers like Salt-N-Pepa and Sweet Tee. Most of them were rocking door knocker earrings, colorful leather jackets, and intricate hi-lo haircuts. They looked fly. And there I was in my long, unstylish skirts. My mom was still trying to salvage what was left of my thick, long hair after a brief stint with a Jheri curl in middle school, so there was no way she was about to let me try something like an asymmetrical haircut or bleached hair. But what I did get was a bad attitude. And I decided to let it work overtime to fill the deficit I felt from not having the rest.

I had tested into a number of honors and advanced courses, so I spent most of my day with a group of kids who fit somewhere between eager nerd or naturally smart with an attitude (like me)—or they were just white. My homeroom was a different story. Every morning we reported to a random classroom with no agenda besides listening to garbled announcements and having our attendance taken. The students in my homeroom were unruly. As a recent Catholic school student, it was beyond my comprehension that kids would be so rude and disrespectful to a teacher. I mean, we got a little hype back at Sacred Heart Middle School, but cursing at a teacher? Not listening at all? Walking in and out of the classroom? Unheard of.

My freshman homeroom was wild. Outside of some random name calling, I had never actually been bullied, but the girls in my homeroom started making comments about my wearing skirts daily. After about a week of taunting, I called on my Aunt Cecelia, my mother's younger sister, who functioned more like an older sister to me than an aunt. She was the flyest person I knew and, outside of my mother and grandmother, definitely the toughest. If there was ever some kind of beef or argument and you heard her loudly say, "*I know* one *thing . . .* ," it was wise to pay close attention to that *one* thing if you wanted to save yourself some grief.

I explained the homeroom situation to my aunt, who was also trying to convince my mom to reverse her skirt rule. She looked me dead in the eyes and said, "never let them see you sweat." It was advice I'd hear from her again and again. She told me to practice saying one phrase with force, so that everyone in earshot believed me: "*Fuck you!*" Even if I were scared, she said, my mouth could usually get me out of a tight corner if I was loud and convincing enough.

"But you *always* have to be prepared to fight," my aunt warned. I thought of my mom's street advice. Ever since I had been jumped by three girls on my way home in the fourth grade, my mom would tell me that if it ever happened again to pick the one with the biggest mouth, punch her in the face or kick her in the coochie, and then just keep beating on her and don't let go. She assured me that my granddaddy had given her the same advice, and it always worked.

A month later, one of the girls from my homeroom stole my purse. It was a very good knockoff Gucci that my Uncle Joey had taken me to Southern Boulevard to purchase as a late birthday gift. Not only did the girl steal the bag off my desk when I wasn't looking, she came to homeroom the next day carrying the purse with my stuff still inside. I politely asked her if it was my purse.

She jumped up and started screaming. "You calling me a thief? You saying I stole from you?" Before I could get my bearings, she took a swing at me. She was a tall girl, probably five-ten to my five-five. When her swing missed, my instincts kicked in. I jumped up on my desk, and when she came lunging at me again I popped her dead in the mouth with my fist, which caught everyone—especially the girl—by surprise. She fell back and tried to come at me again, but the teacher grabbed her and restrained her arms.

And then she spat at me.

I had been spat at before. In elementary school, a girl I bullied because I was jealous that my friend liked her better spat on me during an argument. I beat her up, kinda. The fight was over as quickly as it started. Mr. Wes came up to the school to get me. When I got home, he asked me why I had been fighting. I told him a girl had spat on me, and he seemed satisfied with that response. I could hear my mom fussing over the phone when he called to tell her I had gotten in trouble for fighting. I heard him say, "The girl spit on her . . ." My mother went ballistic on the other end. Spitting on or at someone is one of the worst forms of disrespect in the Black community. No way would my mother tolerate it happening to her child. I didn't get in trouble for my bullying or the fight it caused. Instead, my mother lectured me that if anyone ever opened their mouth to spit on me, I should try to rip their tongue out.

When the girl in homeroom spat on me, something snapped. The good-girl wall that I had been slowly chipping away at finally crumbled, and I proceeded to whup her ass as the teacher struggled to regain control of the situation. Security guards were called into the classroom to assist, and we were both taken to the principal's office. I got off with an in-school suspension once it was revealed that the other girl had both stolen my purse and swung at me first. I was a stellar student on paper, but the principal warned me not to fall into bad habits like violence. I had to hold my tongue not to say *how can I not make violence a habit when I am surrounded by it?*

But something else was happening at the same time. For once, I felt powerful. I felt strong. Maybe even a little free. Someone tried me and I had an immediate response. I liked that. I needed that. My whole existence in Catholic school had been dependent on being a "good girl." But that day, my rage showed up and the shame disappeared.

That school year there were at least six more fights—most defending other people or myself—and seven more suspensions—in and out of school. A new persona emerged. The girl who was so afraid of everything in middle school had found a way to be fearless, and it felt good.

My year at Truman was a roller-coaster ride. I started out wide-eyed and unaware, and then once I was forced to defend myself and fight back I felt powerful. But this power came with overwhelming anxiety. All of the time. I was anxious about getting into the next fight. I was anxious about getting caught. I was anxious about running with a crowd I knew my mom wouldn't approve of. I was anxious that my grades would slip. And, most of all, I was anxious that somehow, some way, these folks would find out that I was a fraud. I rejected close friendships with the other girls in my honors classes and instead opted for a band of, what some might call, misfits. I felt like myself around them or at least part of myself.

There was a boy in our crew who was always joking around and flirting with me. From the way he cozied up to me, I knew he liked me. I didn't know if I liked him, but I liked being liked. Sometimes we'd kiss and he'd feel me up. It was just stupid stuff to the rest of our crew, but it was a big deal to me. No boy had ever touched me with my permission or expressed desire before. I liked it but not enough to let things go further when he asked. I was just trying this new feeling out.

I met up with my crew one day in my friend's apartment, and something was decidedly different. No one would make eye contact with me, but there seemed to be a whole conversation taking place behind the looks they all shot at each other. Finally, one of them took me aside and explained that another one of our friends, who we called Little Stephanie, has slept with King, the guy I'd been hanging around, before I got there. She'd had actual sex with him—*my* him. The boy I had convinced myself I liked. The boy I had let kiss me and feel on me.

My friends all sat there quietly as I put it all together, and then one of them said, "She's here. We made her stay until you got here." He was gone, but she was there. And instead of yelling and screaming at him I settled for beating her up, badly. I wasn't even mad at her, really, but the crew hyped me up. They'd made her stay because they wanted this to happen.

She just sat there pitifully, begging to explain how it happened. I was too young and impressionable to ask the right questions. I had been summoned to perform by my friends, and I didn't want to disappoint. I went at her hard, fighting like she had hit my mother. I beat her into the hallway and then chased her downstairs and out of the building, where I fought her again. She left with the wire from her braces sticking through her lip. It was awful. And worse, every single person in the crew was cheering me on as I beat her ass. People who she woke up thinking were her friends. She kept saying sorry as she tried to defend herself. She never fought back and never shifted from an apologetic posture, no matter how hard I hit her or how much venom I spit at her.

I was tired when the fight was over. I went home as if nothing happened, barely marked from the brawl. I wrote in my journal that night about the fight and all that happened earlier in the day, still in my teenage ego bubble. What I didn't write in the midst of my bragging and shit-talking about how much blood there was and how scared she looked was how relieved I was. I didn't talk about the weight that was lifted by thinking that if she was having sex with him, it meant I was off the hook. And if I was off the hook, it meant I didn't have to tell anyone what had happened to me. She didn't have the same luck with her secrets. The next day in school I met up with my friends to go to lunch, and we saw her sitting alone in the cafeteria.

"Look at that ho! Don't nobody want to eat with a skeezer!" one friend yelled loud enough for a good portion of the students to turn and look in her direction. I laughed, but not too hard. We were more similar than any of our supposed friends knew.

It wasn't until many years later that a question popped into my head when retelling this story to a new group of friends. I was recalling the extent of my "wild youth," talking about how crazy I went on this girl. But it made me remember something else. It made me remember just how handsy that guy had been when we were alone. My relief that she had sex with him came from knowing that he was probably not going to be satisfied until I had sex with him. He didn't seem like the type who took no for an answer for long—and maybe he hadn't. The question I wish I knew to ask at the time was: *Did you say yes?* It gave me such a sinking feeling to think that this poor girl might have been forced to have sex, raped in a house full of people, and then held while they waited patiently to bait me into beating the hell out of her. It's the trap in which so many Black girls find themselves, either performing our pain or performing through it.

I grew up listening to my mother's copy of the Broadway production of *For Colored Girls Who Have Considered Suicide/ When the Rainbow Is Enuf* by Ntozake Shange. My mom listened to it so much that I had memorized a good chunk of it by the time I was in middle school. In one of the final pieces, "a nite with beau willie brown," performed by the Lady in Red, there is a line repeated in the poem: "there was no air." I was captivated by that line. I would say it over and over again. I didn't know why but each time it felt like a small release. Growing up, I had a short list of emotions to cycle through: happy, sad, fear, and anger. I couldn't quite grasp the other ones: shame, grief, vulnerability, and emotional pain. I didn't understand anxiety, so I had no way to explain the fluttering in my chest and rock-hard feeling in my stomach that paralyzed me at any given moment. I didn't understand why I had to keep these things to myself; I just knew I had to. I had to keep performing. And there was no air—for me, a dark-skinned Black girl who had been damaged and used. There was no air for me to be anything but what "they" said I was. Girls like me didn't get the air to cry, the air to release our shame—the air to say, *I don't want to fight you. I don't even know why I'm so mad at you except for that you look like me, and who the fuck am I?* We didn't get the air to be reborn and handled warmly.

sunshine and rain

For all the chaos that happened at Truman, my honors classes were a place I could flex my smarts and not have to be on defense all the time. I spoke up and gave my opinion, and it was rewarded. Doing my homework and scoring well on exams and papers became an easy substitute for praying the rosary. I didn't have to constantly think about what everyone else might be thinking of me. I still felt the unsettling presence of my two selves, but the more I walked in this role the more it felt like the real me.

My favorite class was Honors English. My mother was the reason that I fell in love with literature. Our home was a Black woman's literary paradise. She had hundreds of books all over our house, and a majority of them were by the most beloved and revered Black women writers of our lifetime. Toni Morrison and Alice Walker, Gwendolyn Brooks and Ntozake Shange, Nikki Giovanni and Maya Angelou, among others. I was drawn in by the pretty covers and spectacular titles. Maya Angelou's books, in particular, were dazzling and inviting, but every time I asked my mom if I could read one she would say I wasn't ready. I obeyed her and left the books alone, but my curiosity only grew.

One day, while my mom was out of the house, I couldn't help myself. I snuck her copy of *I Know Why the Caged Bird Sings* off the shelf. I had to have been around twelve. I had assumed my mother held me back from reading the book because she thought it would be too difficult to understand, but the words came easy. It didn't take long before I was hooked.

Reading the opening chapter about young Maya running out of the church peeing on herself reminded me of a similarly embarrassing moment in my own life. There was something so strangely comforting about reading how she laughed at her embarrassment, even though she knew the adults would punish her and the other kids would tease her. I found myself wishing that I was her friend so that I could learn to laugh at myself too, even when I was scared. I kept reading, fascinated by the way she talked about her thoughts and emotions, and how many of them mirrored how I felt about myself.

And then Mr. Freeman was introduced.

I understand now why my mother might have been wary of my reading this book too soon. Maya Angelou wrote of being molested and raped by her mother's boyfriend when she was eight years old. My mom, who had no idea that my life was being mirrored in this book, likely didn't want me to read it in an attempt to protect me from an ugly reality I had unfortunately already experienced. Instead of being horrified and compelled to ask incessant questions, I was being introduced to a truth that would forever alter my life. My twelve-year-old mind had not understood that this was a thing that happened to *other* girls who were innocent. I thought it was just me, or at least girls *like* me. I thought I was the *kind* of girl who bad things happened to. When I read about what happened to a young Maya Angelou, I was able to read her as innocent in a way I didn't allow of myself. Maya was decent and nice, and it seemed egregious that God would have allowed something so horrible to happen to her. It was the first time I ever realized a little girl like her could have gone through what I went through.

I finished the book and kept what was now, in my mind, our secret. To my twelve-year-old self, Maya Angelou was just another name on my mother's bookshelf. She wasn't Dr. Maya Angelou, the esteemed poet, author, activist, and all-around legend—she was a lady who wrote a book that shared my secrets. She was my confidant. I no longer felt alone.

By the time I was in high school, my love for Maya Angelou and her work had only grown, so I was excited when we were assigned to read and interpret her landmark poem "Phenomenal Woman" in my Honors English class.

My teacher, Mr. Pete, was a roundish, middle-aged white man with a dirty blond comb-over and an unkempt, bushy mustache. He was more partial to tweed car coats and brogans than the khakis and polo shirts his fellow male teachers wore. I remember him always smelling of old deli meat, but he prided himself on thinking outside the box and didn't seem jaded by the daily barrage of brown faces like many of his contemporaries. He prided himself on coming up with new and inventive ways for us to learn, and when he thought he was connecting with us a sly smirk would creep across his face and he'd start walking with a little bop in his step, basking in his white liberal glory.

The day he introduced "Phenomenal Woman" to the class was one of his "glory days." He passed out the handout, saying, "You guys are *so* going to love this!" He seemed very proud of himself for having the poem in his Black History Month curriculum. Most of the class didn't know the poem, and many didn't know who Mama Maya was, but a jolt of excitement went through my body when I saw her name on the paper. My hand shot up to volunteer when Mr. Pete asked for someone to read the poem out loud.

A classmate and I took turns. My body was buzzing the whole time. My worlds were colliding—I even caught myself wishing my mom was there to watch me. I was in full performance mode. I took my time with each phrase, acting it out and overenunciating. I wanted my classmates to laugh, but more than anything I was proud to be speaking *her* words.

When we were finished, Mr. Pete thanked us for reading and turned to the rest of the class. "What do you think this poem is about?"

Someone quickly raised their hand. Barely waiting to be called on, they said, "it's about her letting the world know that she was fly."

The class laughed, and Mr. Pete nodded vigorously, using the student's comment to launch into his own interpretation. "It was her way of saying 'Hey world, look at me, I'm a Black woman and I'm just as good as any white woman!'"

His comment irritated me a little bit, but I couldn't quite pinpoint why. He quieted the class and put on a videotape of Dr. Angelou reciting the poem. Then it hit me.

The entire class sat intently listening to the performance, but I was holding my breath. In all the time I had spent being enamored by her life, her strength, and her words, I had never actually heard her voice. Her regal tone and accent and protracted enunciation were unlike anything I had ever heard from a Black woman. It was completely unfamiliar to me, and I was mesmerized. She stood at a podium wearing a black-and-silver dress, with the broadest, warmest smile on her face. She made little jokes that sent flickers of laughter across the audience. She rolled her tongue and lowered her tone and pronounced every single word as if each one was her own invention.

She was absolutely divine.

My mother's all-time favorite artist is Patti LaBelle. I always thought of her presence as big, grand, and *divine*—because of her big hair and sparkling clothes and that booming voice that commanded your attention. Here was Dr. Angelou standing at a podium and, though beautifully dressed, she was using nothing but words to command such a presence.

When the performance was done, Mr. Pete stopped the recording and went into that weird ditty-bop movement he liked to do. "She's talking jive, right? She's kinda trash-talking and saying, 'Yeah I'm better than you and you better believe it!'" He said all this with his smug smirk, mocking jive talk in the ridiculous way only a white person would.

My breath came back to me all at once. "What are you talking about? No!"

Mr. Pete turned to me calmly—he was used to my out-bursts—and gestured for me to continue. "Okay, Ta-raan-a, elaborate." He always pronounced my name wrong, no matter how often I corrected him, saying *ran* in the middle instead of *ron*. It worked my nerves. I might not have known the term *microaggression* then, but I was old enough to peep that he was doing that shit on purpose.

I leaned forward in my seat, my words slow and delib-erate, trying to walk back my attitude. "Maya Angelou was talking about appreciating who she was as a Black woman because nobody else would. She wasn't 'jive talkin' or com-paring herself to white women. All Black women should feel the way she felt in the poem because we are all QUEENS. She never once mentioned white women or being white at all."

I was passionate about my response. It was just like a white man to open his mouth and believe she *had* to be talking about them, and I wasn't having it. I kept going. "This poem is powerful because she is powerful, and we're not even talking about all of the stuff she's been through," I explained. "This is a poem about a Black woman making sure the world understands that she is not defeated despite what they may think of her."

When I was done, the class was silent except for a few awkward snickers. My classmates' reactions ranged from annoyed to awed to amused.

Mr. Pete gave a halfhearted apology for offending me and anyone else in the class and then went on to give a long, drawn-out lesson on the history of "jive talk" in America. I rolled my eyes.

As I sat tuning out my teacher, my mind returned to what I had just seen—how had a woman who had been through what I'd been through been able to claim such confidence and pride? I asked to be excused to the restroom and walked down the hall until I got to the one stairwell that wasn't constantly overrun with kids. I sat down, stunned by how badly I wanted to both scream and cry.

Everything I knew and held sacred in my memory of young Maya Angelou and what happened to her was smacking up against what I had just heard. And even though I stood up in class and defended her right to be "phenomenal," intellectually, I didn't understand what that meant or how it was even possible emotionally. While I was finding newfound comfort in anger, she was smiling. While I was lashing out, she was laughing and reciting beautiful poetry. Why wasn't she *mad*? Why wasn't she cursing and spitting at white folks and everyone else?

I was suddenly staring my duality in the face. Because of Maya Angelou's words, maybe I didn't have to be either that dirty, nasty, fast girl or the perfect little Catholic girl. Maybe I could just be a Black Queen like all of the conscious hip-hop songs said I was. Even if I didn't believe it all the time, Maya Angelou had given me a model for how to step out into the world and make them believe it. Before, I had thought she was giving me a road map for how to "go along to get along" or "fake it till you make it." I was convinced that she lived a dual life like my own. But when she opened her mouth, none of that proved to be true. Listening to her voice, watching her lips perfectly articulate each and every syllable of that poem, I knew she meant every word.

I believed her.

I believed that she felt like a Phenomenal Woman as she delivered each line with an audacity and authenticity I had never seen before. I felt like I knew the kind of pain she had to be holding because it was the same pain I held every single day. Where had her shame gone? How had it not seeped into her cells, and if it had, how did she get it out? And if all of it—the pain, shame, and fear—were still there, where did she find space for this thing I saw in her face and heard in her voice? What was this softness? Where did the joy come from? I went home that night and wondered in my journal who Dr. Maya Angelou was—for real—and how I could have gotten her so wrong.

More than anything, I contemplated the question that eventually became central to my healing. If what I saw was real, how could a body that holds that kind of pain also hold joy?

fight the power

I only spent one year at Truman. After all the fights, suspensions, and shenanigans, my mother decided that she needed to get me out. New York City has something called a safety transfer that allows students to move schools when there is a fear of harm. With the number of fights I'd had, I qualified, but that didn't stop the principal from trying to block me from leaving. He said I was an asset to the Honor Bowl team. My mother had grown weary of my disciplinary meetings and was not going to let this man stand in her way. Like most households run by a single matriarch, she ran a tight ship and rarely, if ever, missed a day of work. She simply couldn't afford to. So she marched into his office and gave him a piece of her mind, and days later I was allowed to transfer to Herbert H. Lehman High School.

Lehman fancied itself as one of the better schools in the Bronx. It had computer labs and newish science labs. The student body was about 60 percent white. Back then, the zoning laws dictated that 90 percent of the student body of any high school, except special admission schools and a few others, come from the community where the school was located. Lehman is situated in an area of the Bronx called Throggs Neck, where despite the borough's high population of Black and Latinx folks, a vast majority of white ethnic groups reside, mostly Italian, Albanian, Polish, and Irish. But right at the end of the zone, tucked away past the rows of privately owned homes, were the Throggs Neck Houses. That's where most of the limited number of Black and Brown folks at the school lived. My great-grandmother lived there too, and her address helped secure my transfer to the school.

Transferring felt like another chance to reinvent myself. I didn't want to fight. I didn't want to cut class. I wanted to lean into the "me" I had caught a glimpse of the day we read "Phenomenal Woman" in class. My honors classes were predominately white, as were most of the teachers at the school. There were few activities for Black and Brown students, and I found myself challenging students and teachers alike about issues in the media or around the school.

In my tenth grade Global History class, Ms. Magi was teaching us about Africa and what we now call the Middle

East. My ears perked up when she mentioned that Jesus Christ was from this part of the world. I couldn't help but raise my hand.

"Tarana, you have a question?" It was a question, but her tone made it sound like an obvious statement.

"Yeah," I replied. "If Jesus is from this area, how come white people always depict him with blond hair and blue eyes? Clearly he looked more like us than he did like y'all."

There was a collective groan. One of the boys said, "Oh boy, here goes Farrakhan over here."

The class erupted in laughter. I did not. I turned around in my seat, looking at the whole class.

"Hair like lamb's wool and bronzed skin. He was an AFRICAN!" I said, emphasizing every syllable.

Another boy gave me a snide look. "So you're saying Jesus was a . . ." He trailed off but not before Ms. Magi jumped in.

"*All right*, enough!"

I was already up and out of my seat, face hot. "What were you going to say?!"

We went back and forth like this while Ms. Magi, who was about three apples tall, desperately tried to regain control. In a final plea, she pulled out the demerit cards, which meant detention, and we fell silent.

She let out a huff and looked directly at me. "For the record, while Jesus probably didn't look like the pictures of him that we traditionally see, he was not from sub-Saharan Africa, so technically he would not be considered African."

I was only fifteen, but this big, African nose could smell white supremacy from a mile away. She just couldn't let that white boy be wrong. She couldn't let Africa tarnish Jesus's good name before sending these honor students into their impending lifelong mediocrity. She, a history teacher, couched her racism in such a cowardly place that I said the only thing I could muster up.

"Get the FUCK outta here!"

I, of course, was immediately sent to the principal's office, but I didn't care. My granddaddy had been preparing me for this since I was in elementary school. I easily settled into my new reputation as the "Black Power girl."

I quickly found my lane at Lehman. I joined the track team—which I had quit at Truman, even though I had been running since I was six years old. The team gave me friends and a place to belong, but it also threw me into a mix of social dynamics and style jockeying. It was the late '80s, and if you weren't wearing Guess or Girbaud jeans or North Face or a Triple F.A.T. Goose coat, you might as well keep your ass at home. I had none of those, of course. My mother was not having it, and I didn't have my own job or money. She wasn't going to spend a grip on clothes for school because she didn't have a grip to spend—but she did, at least, finally have the presence of mind to want me to fit in. I loved her for wanting to help, but in high school I would have rather worn a sackcloth to school than designer knockoff clothes. I wish I'd had the courage to say it before she conspired with my aunt down south, who sent me a pair of Chic jeans from Target. My granddaddy also took me to Lerner's, where I got a low-backed top for my birthday.

I was obsessive about covering my body in high school. I tried my best to ignore whatever was happening with my butt and breasts. A pair of fitted jeans and a low-back top were a complete shift for me, but I finally felt cute. I put on my new outfit and headed to the skating rink with my girlfriends. As I skated around the rink I felt normal—which was rare—and I beamed with confidence the whole time. The night was going great, but as we were leaving a fight broke out. When shots rang out, my girls and I took off running with a group of other kids toward the train station, not stopping to catch our breaths until we were far enough away from the chaos. By now, most of the crowd had gone off in separate directions, but some of the boys stuck around. Boys made me nervous. I never knew how it was going to go or what they wanted from me so I either froze, or got loud and agitated, or shrunk inside myself. One of the dudes came up behind me and ran his finger down my back, collecting some of the sweat that had accumulated during the mad dash to safety. His touch startled me, and I jumped and turned to look at him just as he was backing up with both hands in the air.

"Sorry, ma." He laughed. "You turned around like you was gonna punch me in the face or something. I was just getting the sweat off ya back."

"But you touched me!" I snapped, wishing I had just gone with being quiet.

"Oh, I can't touch you? That's what you saying." He chuckled as he let me turn around and then proceeded to put his whole hand on my back.

"Yo! Cut it out!" I shouted. I didn't want to fight, and I didn't know if these dudes were the *I fight girls* kind or not. Plus, he was kind of cute, and I was still feeling fresh from the night. I softened my stance, or tried my best.

"How you just putting your hands on me without permission like that?" I said as coyly as I could muster.

"Oh, I'm sorry. Can I put my hands on you, miss? *How 'bout like this,*" he said as he slid his arm around my neck, making a flash of heat spread over my skin. We walked together for a bit, him asking questions and me trying to be casual. I was *just* starting to feel a little relaxed when I heard a voice from behind us call out.

"Ay yo—what the fuck kind of jeans she got on?" My body froze, but my heartbeat quickened. My new friend stopped to turn around, and in that moment I knew I was done for. Before I could walk away he fell back a step, bent over, and read my jean label.

"YO! CHIC JEANS," he yelled to his friends incredulously. "*She got on CHIC jeans!*" He squealed again. I started walking faster, but he caught right up.

"So, you got on Chic. Jeans. Damn! Where did you find those in the first place?"

I kept walking and looking straight ahead.

"Did you think you would get away with it? I'm curious."

I kept quiet, put my head down, and concentrated on walking.

"I mean you could have even rocked a Jordache or a Lee jean and got away with it, but *CHIC* jeans, ma. That's a violation. You know that, right?" He seemed so genuine in his incredulity. So genuine that I couldn't even be mad.

"Yeah, *I know,*" I said with a sigh that made him laugh.

"Someone made you wear those, right? I know that's what happened. Your moms, right?"

I nodded in agreement, letting myself laugh with him. His boys were still yelling at him to tell them more about this girl who played herself by wearing Chic jeans. To my surprise he yelled back for them to chill.

"Listen," he said, turning back to me. "Once my moms tried to make me wear some fake-ass shell toes from Fayva!"

I snickered.

"Yeah, I wore them shits one time and was plotting the whole time on how I was going to get my own one day. I ain't asked my mom to buy me kicks since! I got me a job. I buy my own shit."

I smiled at him gratefully. "My mother won't let me get a job. She says it would be bad for my schoolwork or something."

He nodded understandingly, agreeing that schoolwork should come first.

"Get you a nigga that's hustlin'. He can buy you shit," he said, now fully committed to helping me solve this life dilemma of not being wack in public.

"I can't accept gifts from boys," I said.

"Damn. Well, ma, you got a fat ass so that will help a little bit if you gotta wear these Chic ass jeans, but maybe get a long shirt or sweater so nobody can read the back. Cause they mad wack." He shot me a "just saying" glance. I was so grateful to him for not blowing me up and told him as much.

"No problem," he said. "You sweet and I can tell you smart. I like a smart girl." And then, just as I was allowing myself to blush a wee bit he said, "But I can't give you my number cuz you *do* have them Chic ass jeans on! Ahhhhhhhhhh!"

He laughed, running off to join his friends. I jokingly yelled "shut *up*!" after him, but I wasn't even mad. He turned back and gave me a salute and caught up with his boys. I stood at the bottom of the steps at the train station and waited for my friends to catch up to me, then recounted the whole story. On the ride home I decided it was time to get a job and some of my own money, no matter what my mom said.

My high school had a dropout prevention program that we called the "jobs office" because they helped teens find work that gave them school credits, and I started hanging around the office before track practice. My mom was still paranoid about a job taking time away from school, but I was desperate. I'd find a way to convince her.

I was hanging around one day, trying not to look too out of place, when Mr. Ayala, who managed the office, spotted me.

As if he could read my mind he asked me, "Have you ever thought about working here? You're here all the time anyway, and you know the filing system and the students," he offered. "And you are *always* here anyway."

I don't think I ever said yes to something so fast in my life. The deal was that I could work in the office during my daily free period and three times a week after school. I went home that night and made a hard sell to my mom. I rambled about all the perks and mentoring and college trips they were planning until I ran out of information. She finally relented—I wasn't asking for money, after all—but under one condition: "I better not see a single grade drop. Not even a point, you hear me?"

I made whatever promise I had to make to get her to sign that paper and went to school the next day elated. I was now making minimum wage, which was somewhere around $3.50 an hour then. Every two weeks I got a check for between thirty to fifty dollars, but it might as well have been a thousand dollars. But more than the money, I loved working. I loved being useful, and so I threw myself into it. Mr. Ayala would walk by me and smile, chuckling to himself as I furiously filed and did whatever mundane office task I'd been assigned with determination. One day he stopped instead of walking on by.

"You know my boss, David Harris? He's the executive director of Jobs for Youth. He was asking if there was a student I might want to send along on a leadership development trip to Washington, DC, this spring." He raised his eyebrows at me. I didn't let a beat pass before I eagerly agreed. Mr. Ayala asked me to think of some other students who might want to go as well. I promised that I would, but my mind was already thinking about how to get a "yes" from my mother.

Every major ask in my house, especially those that involved money, required carefully planned stages. The first stage was the literal ask. This involved finding the precise time to come to my mother with the question. It could never be when she just got home from work, because she walked in the door executing a to-do list while simultaneously commencing a home inspection. It couldn't be during any of her favorite shows, because she would be only half listening and it would annoy her that I was disrupting her TV time. Those times were the easiest to avoid, but the third was the trickiest and required a great deal of skill, patience, and intuition. The ask also couldn't be when she was in a "mood." Not just a bad mood—any mood, really. If I asked when she was mad, that was asking for a rejection and subjecting myself to scrutiny on other arbitrary things she picked out of thin air. If I asked when she was in a really good mood, I could easily turn her mood because she might think I was trying to take advantage of it. If I asked when she was money mad—which meant when she was looking at bills, opening mail with bills, or dealing with some other cash-related matter that irritated her—I might get a silent death stare, which could be accompanied by the kind of yelling that wakes your ancestors. Or I'd get the silent, nonnegotiable, immovable "no."

It was scary territory to navigate, but I'd learned a few things as a teenager. I had even invented my own special strategy. I had learned to create a mood. I'd pick a neutral moment and share some story (real or invented) that we could both be frustrated about. Telling her some stupid shit a white person did always riled her up. *"Ma, you not going to believe what this white lady did on the bus on the way home today!"* Or, I'd ask her for help with some schoolwork that wasn't hard enough to frustrate her or easy enough to make her think I was stupid. It would make her feel useful. *"Ma, did you ever read about the Moors? Did you know they were Black?!"*

That night, I was lucky to quickly get past Phase One with a simple homework question. Now for Phase Two: money. Is this ask going to cost anything? This phase moves rather quickly, but I still had to be ready with answers to questions that came in rapid fire.

"How much does it cost?"

"Free."

"Nothing is free. What about food?"

"It's included."

"All your food for a whole weekend? How are you getting there?"

"On a charter bus."

"Well, who is paying for that?"

"They are."

"Who is *they*?"

"My school program."

"What about when the bus stops?"

"I'll pack food."

"You packing *my* food that *I* paid for?"

"I have some money. I can buy a hero."

"You *better* use your own money. Where are you going exactly?"

That is when I knew Phase Three was close, when she moved from money to details. I had her, and I was ready.

"It's in Chevy Chase, Maryland. There will be a bunch of kids from my school and other schools. We are staying at the 4-H Center. We are leaving from in front of the school on Friday morning and coming back on Sunday afternoon. There will be three students to a room and a counselor on each floor."

"Where will the boys be?"

"Separated," I lied. I didn't know, but I had to respond in kind to every question. One good *ummm* would put me back to Phase One.

"Here is the paperwork and the permission slip. And Mr. Ayala said you can call him at the number on the paper to ask any questions."

Silence while she skimmed over the paperwork.

Deep sigh.

"When do you have to know?"

This was a trick question. She was always trying to trip me up one last time. The biggest part of the strategy was timing. I couldn't ask too far in advance because I'd risk getting put on punishment for some dumb thing and having the trip revoked. I also couldn't ask within two or three days of the trip because it would be an automatic no. I gave her the best answer I had in the moment. "Soon."

"Okay, I'll let you know," she finally said.

"Thank you, Mommy," I said as I turned on my heels, smiling to myself. There was one phase left, but by this time I was pretty sure I'd get to go.

The last phase was the wait. Once I got a preliminary yes, there was about a one-week waiting period. Two or three days later, she made the call for more information and to confirm everything I told her. Then I got the permission slip. Then there was about a three-day period, usually over a weekend, where I was in limbo and on my best behavior because *any little slip-up* could get the trip revoked. In my mother's house, you didn't actually know if you were going until the day you left. But I made it. I made it on that trip, and it was worth every one of those phases. My life would never be the same.

what shall i give?

The youth leadership trip to Washington, DC, represented many firsts for me: I had never been on an overnight school trip, I had never been to DC before, and I had never met and mingled with kids from schools in Brooklyn and Manhattan outside of track meets. We met up with the other New York students only moments before we met with the students from other states. They lined us up in the cafeteria to give us rules and room assignments and lectures about behavior. I was starting to get antsy because I could hear music coming from some other place on campus and I wanted to know where. When the formalities were over, they informed us that we were going to a pep rally. We crossed the yard and filed slowly into another building. As we got closer, the music got louder. I could make out a piano playing and drums backing it up. I asked my friend if she thought it was a show or something and she just shrugged her shoulders. And then the doors opened. The music came blasting forward like a gust of wind, catching us all by surprise. We slowed our steps, moving into the large room more cautiously, but the drum beats and the sound of kids singing at the top of their lungs beckoned us.

We walked into the room to find kids singing loudly and dancing both in and on their seats to the djembe drums. Our school pep rallies were nothing like this. We had maybe two a year, and they consisted of our majority white cheerleaders cheering as the football team came running into the auditorium. They got a little rowdy when the most popular players came in, or when we finally got Black cheerleaders. But I had never seen anything like what was going on in this room. No one was afraid to smile big or sing loud to music that was not on the radio. All of them were locking arms and hugging and jumping around joyously, not caring who looked on. These kids were free. This air was rare. There was magic in that room, and I didn't know what to do with it.

I was standing there, trying to figure out who I was meant to be in the midst of all this freedom when a raspy voice came bellowing out of the crowd and a woman emerged. She was smaller than her voice suggested, but she had a ferocious look in her eyes. Although I had never met her before, I *knew* this woman, or women like her. Her hair was a mess of grown-out braids that were forming locs, sprinkled with random cowrie shells and ornaments, and wrestled back with a Kente-print scrunchie. A single loc had escaped the scrunchie and was dangling in her face, the shell at the end of it whipping back and forth as she moved. She had on a bright T-shirt and Ankara-print harem pants, and her arms were covered almost to her elbows with colorful beaded South African bangles.

"AGOOOOO!!" she screamed, as loud as her deep, earthy voice would allow before it jumped to high falsetto.

The kids all stopped in place and returned her call with a booming, collective voice.

"AMEEEEE!"

I had heard this call and response as a child in African dance classes, but it was never like this. Our group of new-comers stood in the back of the room, buzzing with energy but not quite sure how we fit in just yet.

"AGOOOOOOOO!!!" This time her voice had even more energy, fueled by the response from the crowd.

The young people responded even louder. "AMEEEEEEEE!!"

A silence fell over the entire room and the kids settled in their chairs. We all waited for what was to come next.

The organization that had sponsored this trip, 21st Century Youth Leadership Movement, was founded four years earlier, in 1985, by veterans of the various move-ments of the '60s and '70s: Civil Rights, Black Power, labor, anti-apartheid, and farm cooperatives, among others. Its founding had come out of the twenty-fifth anniversary of the Selma voting rights movement. Every year, the leaders

and foot soldiers of that movement came back to commemorate the watershed moment and the events surrounding it,
including Bloody Sunday. The struggle in Selma didn't result
only in the right to vote for Black people in America; it laid
the foundation for movements in other areas like co-ops,
labor, and Black Power. The founding activists and organizers, who were advancing in age and wisdom, wanted to be
sure the next generation picked up the mantle of the work
they had started.

A small but mighty group, affectionately dubbed "The
Elders," had helped start the organization, but really the
whole thing was the brainchild of a woman named Faya Rose
Mary Touré Sanders. She was the woman with the booming voice. Everyone called her Rose Sanders, Mrs. Sanders,
or Faya when she legally changed her name after surviving
breast cancer. She was a partner in the largest Black law firm
in Alabama, cofounded with her husband Hank "The Rock"
Sanders, a powerful state senator, along with friend and legendary attorney J. L. Chestnut Jr., who had been a part of
Dr. King's Alabama legal team. Mrs. Sanders was unlike any
other adult I had ever met in my life. Right then, as I sat listening to her, I knew this was going to change my life.

The New York students didn't sing along or stand and
clap. We just sat back taking it all in. Some folks cracked
jokes. Others had an attitude about all of the free-spirited-
ness. I wondered if others were like me, having a hard time
not letting their hearts burst wide open.

Mrs. Sanders called for us to get up out of our seats and
stand for *the pledge.* I had no idea what she meant—I knew
that I was not about to recite the Pledge of Allegiance—but

I stood, reluctantly. Mrs. Sanders came off the stage and marched right toward our group. There were at least eighty of us, fresh off the streets of New York, with little exposure to much other than the city and holding down a reputation for bad attitudes.

"I want to welcome the young people from New York in the room. Let's give them a round of applause!" The rest of the kids broke out into wild clapping and screaming while we stood silently, wondering what she'd say next. I felt a warm feeling creeping into my heart and spreading over my whole spirit.

She turned back to face us. "I know you are looking at us, saying, *What are these ALABAMA kids doing?!* Right?" A few heads nodded. Others snickered. And then she asked,

"How many of you think you are leaders?"

No one responded. I felt the air shift under the weight of all these kids uncomfortably performing their toughness. She left our group and moved back toward the kids from Alabama at the front of the room and repeated the question. Every one of them raised their hands.

"How many of you KNOW you are leaders?"

They started waving their hands around feverishly. Some kids were jumping up like they were going to spontaneously combust if they weren't called on, but she was already moving back down the aisle toward us. She looked directly at us and, with a little more energy, asked again.

"How many of you KNOW that you are a leader?! Come on, New York!"

Some of the kids started looking around at each other, and then to the adults who had brought us there. I never took my eyes off Mrs. Sanders. Everything in my body wanted to raise my hand, and everything in my brain was cautioning me to just be still and not be corny. Mrs. Sanders took her microphone and pointed it at one of the New York students. She instructed him to say, "I am a leader." He barely whispered it. She put her arm around him tenderly and held the microphone close to his face and coached him to repeat it again, but *louder*.

"I am a leader," he said again, only slightly louder.

"Are you sure?"

Other kids from the front of the room jumped in with shouts of "you are!" and "that's right!"

The boy nodded yes, but he was clearly getting agitated. He shifted awkwardly under the weight of her arm, as if it felt like a knife twisting into his shoulder, and gave Mrs. Sanders a resentful look.

She turned so she was facing him directly. She spoke deliberately into the microphone. "I'm sorry to put you on the spot, young man, but I have to let you know. You are here *because* you are a leader. I didn't make you a leader. You were a leader before you got on that bus this morning. You were a leader when you woke up this morning. You are a leader because you are a strong *Black* man. You were born a leader."

She spun on her heel and headed back to the stage, shouting into the microphone that we were all leaders, continuing to hype up the crowd. Everyone's attention followed her, but I watched that boy. I could see his eyes welling up with tears. He was breathing heavily, his nostrils flaring like an angry bull. I knew that feeling. I knew the struggle of bottling up emotions that were just below the surface of our skin, begging to be freed. His friends started mocking him, snapping him out of whatever moment he may have been about to have.

I looked away from the boy, now giving Mrs. Sanders my undivided attention as she instructed us to repeat after her. This was the pledge.

I AM a 21st Century Leader.
I must prepare myself to BE
the very BEST that I can be.
I must prepare my BODY, my SPIRIT,
AND my mind.
AND in time.
I'LL shine.
YOU'LL shine.
WE'LL shine.
And the light of LOVE,
JUSTICE,
AND PEACE
Will shine
in the 21st CENTURY
Like NEVER BEFORE
I AM.
YOU ARE.
WE ARE.
21st CENTURY LEADERS!

Saying those words in the wake of her strong call made me believe them. I had been redefining and reinventing my identity for so long, but these words told me who I was. Who I am. Mrs. Sanders and the other 21st Century elders were the first people to validate me as an organizer, a leader and, in many ways, a survivor. My grandfather and mother grounded me in Black history and Black consciousness, but 21C gave me the tools and courage to use that consciousness to change my community. They trained us to strategize and organize, to recognize and fight against injustice, and to think of ourselves as leaders at any age, whether we were out in front speaking or doing our part in the background.

By the end of that first weekend, we were ready to return to New York and start our own 21st Century chapters. I became fully immersed in the organization, attending every gathering and camp. I was the president of the chapter at Lehman, which only added to my Black Power persona around the school. I was now an organizer, full-blown.

Later that year, a group of five Black boys were accused of assaulting a white woman in Central Park, famously known as the Central Park Jogger case. One of the accused boys, Yusef Salaam, was dating a girl from my school who was also in 21C. We didn't know him well, but the shock of seeing someone we knew, even casually, blasted across the media so viciously was powerful. We discussed the case in our 21C group meetings, talking about how the media had made them out to be criminals and wild savages instead of the kids they were. None of us believed that they had beaten and raped the jogger. Racial tensions in the city were high and the news stoked the fire. Around the same time, a six-teen-year-old Black boy named Yusef Hawkins was killed by a mob of white boys in Bensonhurst, Brooklyn. And then there was the case of Charles Stuart, a white man in Boston who sparked a citywide manhunt for a Black man who had supposedly robbed and murdered his pregnant wife, who he had actually killed. We were all familiar with Black men being falsely accused, and we could not sit by and watch the boys in the Central Park case, or Black youth generally, be shamed and demonized in this vulgar way. I didn't empathize with the jogger as a rape survivor at the time—I connected with the young Black and Brown boys whose lives were being snuffed out simply because their Black and Brown skin made them expendable. The system only cared about finding justice for white victims—by any means. The jogger had never even identified the five Black boys as her attackers. She couldn't, because she had lost all memory of the attack. I didn't think of the trial as a rape trial until much later, when the true rapist was revealed.

Though I was not yet facing the reality of my abuse, I was still actively dealing with the side effects. Standing and fighting against the diminishment and destruction of Black bodies had become a proxy for the diminishment and destruction of my own Black body. Belonging, connecting, and feeling seen and heard allowed me the space to channel my rage and hide my shame, which I more than welcomed.

There were 21st Century chapters all across the world, and many of us spent our formative years coming together to learn, grow, share, and build community. We always convened in Selma, Alabama or at an HBCU in Alabama. My mother started to ease up after she met Mr. Harris, a fellow Bronxite and now my mentor. Everything that 21C was about was in line with how she had been raising me already, so the yeses came much easier for the following trips. And there were plenty. Alabama started to feel like a second home. I didn't have a single blood relation in the state, but I had chosen family, connected not by blood but by love and experience. Even as young people, we held each other up through births, deaths, graduations, dropouts, arrests, breakups, and a whole lot in between.

indelible

By my junior year I had a boyfriend named Sean and had lost my "virginity"—the one of my own free will. We weren't terribly active, but I had done it and used protection each time. My mother found out about it by reading my diary while I was away at my aunt's house in South Carolina for the summer. She did not respond well. She called my aunt, furious and demanding that I come home early. She had no shame in reading my private thoughts and feelings and used the moment to heap more shame on. She acted like she had found the proof she was looking for all those years that I was indeed a dirty, nasty dishrag. At least that is how it made me feel.

She took me to the gynecologist when I got home, without any prep or pep talk. She simply snapped, "Now that you are having sex they have to check you to make sure you don't have any diseases or anything." No nurturing—just shame and judgment. We sat in the gynecologist's office at North Central Hospital in silence. When the nurse came over and told us that the doctor would see me, I stood up. My mother did not. Thinking I had misheard the nurse or moved too soon, I stepped back to sit down, but my mother sniped, "She called your name, not mine."

Usually when I heard my name called at the doctor's office, we went back together. Why was this different? I tried searching my mother's eyes to glean if she was being serious, but my glare was met with that familiar look—stoic, unmoving, and empty. This was her superpower, and she knew it.

"*Go,*" she said, dismissing me to follow the nurse. I was clear that I was going in alone.

The nurse leading me to the room had her hair pulled back into a tight bun and wore a mint-green lab coat. I suddenly missed the fun, colorful nursing jackets the women at the front desk in the pediatric clinic wore. She asked if I was okay as we walked, though she didn't make the usual small talk about school or pop culture like the nurses at my pediatrician's office. She was, however, adept at reading the air and must have sensed the trepidation and nerves building in my chest.

"This your first time?" she inquired with an added gentleness.

"Yes, it is," I confided as we walked the short corridor to the exam room.

I was about to go a step further and tell her that I was actually terrified and didn't know what to expect when she said, "Don't be scared. It's not that bad. It will be a little uncomfortable, but that's a part of being a woman now." I doubt she knew just how prophetic and unnerving those words were.

She instructed me to take off everything except my bra and put on the paper robe that was folded and sitting on the edge of the exam table. She said that when I was done I should sit at the end of the table and that the doctor would be right with me. Then she left. I did as I was told and sat on the table, waiting for whatever was about to happen next.

There was a light knock on the door and the doctor, an older middle-aged white woman, came in and introduced herself. She told me that she would be giving me a pap smear. There was a sternness to her voice as she explained what that was and what they would be testing for. Then she gestured for me to scoot back on the exam table and put my feet in the stirrups.

Sweat had begun collecting on the back of my knees and was seeping into the protective paper beneath me. Reluctantly, I started to scoot back. The paper tore. The doctor didn't hide her agitation as she told me to get up off the table. I awkwardly swung my body to the side and climbed down, clutching the robe closed so as not to expose my butt.

She pulled fresh paper down and smoothed it over the exam table. I wiped the back of my knees and got on the table from the side to eliminate the need to scoot. After my feet were in the stirrups, she instructed me to slide down as far as I could. Now my legs were wide open. Aside from the tissue paper they called a robe, I was almost completely naked. No one had ever seen me this way—not even my boyfriend. Not in shared showers at camp, not while changing between classes or after a track meet. Never. I was *very* careful about this. And now, for reasons I still didn't quite understand, I was basically naked in front of a strange white woman staring into my abyss. She was now taking in something I had never even seen myself. My mind was racing. I was sure that my breathing was heavy and erratic, so I tried to calm down and be quiet. I knew where to go when I was in danger of spilling too much emotion.

The doctor raised her arm to show me what was in her hand and announced each step before she performed it, but it was in no way a preparation for what followed.

One of the worst things about surviving sexual violence—of any kind—is that for a period of time you lose the power to make decisions about your own body. Someone else takes control. Whether they physically wrestle or coerce it away, they take it. It is an indescribably dehumanizing feeling. And for that reason, every decision I made afterward was that much more important. That much more precious. I didn't decide to go to the ob-gyn that day. My mother decided I needed to go. I lay on that table unable to voice my fears, or even ask questions, or pause for a beat between movements. Yes, I had been sexually active. It was my choice and that mattered to me. I was not prepared for this. My mother didn't bother to take two minutes to warn me that a doctor was going to enter me with foreign objects. I lay on that table, afraid and ashamed and embarrassed— and hurt as the doctor prodded me and hit me with a barrage of questions.

"How long have you been sexually active?"

"Not that long," I whispered.

"Good thing your mom brought you in when she did. Do you use condoms?"

"Yes."

"Every time?" she pressed.

"*Yes.*"

Her eyebrows went up slightly, her expression skeptical, when she asked for this confirmation, maintaining eye contact as I twisted my head to see past my bent legs. She launched into a speech about the importance of using condoms, similar to the speeches we were given in health class—the ones where they put a rubber on a banana. I was only half listening. I had become fixated on the navy-blue medical curtain surrounding the examination space. The curtain was attached to a rusting silver pole with common shower curtain rings. They were all sky blue except for the second to last one, which was clear. *Did they think no one would ever notice?* I wondered. How tacky it was to use regular-ass shower curtain rings in a professional doctor's office. I almost got up the gumption to mention it to the jabbering doctor when out of nowhere I felt her finger attempting to enter my anus. I yelped and instinctively squeezed my butt tight. That annoyed the doctor, who had apparently moved from her live condom infomercial to jabbing her index finger into the one orifice in my body that had only ever released.

She pulled her finger out and hissed at me, "I need you to focus. This is no different than what I have already done!"

I turned my head away and bit my bottom lip to keep from saying, *Yes, it is different than what's already been done to me. You put your finger in my booty!* Instead, I told her that it hurt. And she did the thing that so many people have the audacity to do: she corrected my feelings.

"It doesn't *hurt*. It's *uncomfortable*," she insisted. "You can withstand a little *discomfort*."

I lay my head back down and resigned myself to her definition of my experience. I told myself it didn't hurt, but it did. It hurt my head that couldn't keep up with the pace of this moment, and it hurt my heart that was already so battered and bruised. I had learned long ago that silence was my best friend in these moments, so I lay there silently in shame and pain.

When it was done, the doctor told me to get dressed, and she went to chat with my mother. I sat up on the table, took off the paper robe, and began to slowly dress myself. I imagined what she was telling my mother about what had happened. When I came out of the exam room, my mother was filling out paperwork at the front desk.

"You have everything?" she asked as she always did before we left a place.

"Yes, I have all of my stuff."

"Good, let's go."

She returned the clipboard to the desk, and we walked out into the corridor in silence. When we got downstairs, she hailed a cab and we both settled into the back seat. Without meeting my eyes, she asked what had happened, a touch of attitude still in her voice.

"Nothing really," I said casually.

"*Nothing. Really?*" she repeated, turning to look at me.

"I mean she did the tests, and then she asked me questions, and that was it."

"Okay," she replied, as if she wasn't about to push me for more answers.

We rode in silence for another few minutes before I blurted out, "She stuck her finger in my butt!"

My mother burst out laughing. And I did too, but I wasn't really feeling the humor. I was just grateful the tension was broken.

"Yeah, that's all a part of it." She chuckled to herself. "That's what they do!"

I thought the moment of laughter might open up space for conversation, but we fell back into silence for the rest of the ride home.

Later that evening, I overheard my mom talking on the phone with one of her friends about the doctor's appointment. I could only hear parts of the conversation from my bedroom, but she was laughing and saying something about the doctor's wandering fingers. *Why was this funny?* I wondered. And why was the levity always for someone else? We had that outburst in the cab, and it felt for a moment like we might connect or she would explain the lesson in all of this. There had to be a reason she was so mad that went deeper than me experimenting with sex at nearly seventeen years old. But as usual I was left to wonder about it, because all communication between us was either interrogation or delegation. Even without hearing all the words being said, the familiar tone in her voice sent me spiraling backward.

Four years prior, we were in another clinic—not my regular pediatrician but a local clinic in the neighborhood. I was twelve and there was a problem in my private parts. I had developed some kind of rash. There were small sores and it itched terribly. I told my mom and she took a look at it but had no idea what it was. She asked me all manner of questions about where I had been and what I had used down there. We both came up with blanks, except for the fact that I had used the bathroom at Mr. Wes's old apartment the week before, the one my stepsister and her boyfriend had moved into. It was no longer the home I'd lived in during my childhood, but a drug den. They were eventually evicted, and the building supervisor contacted my mom and told her that the apartment was going to be rented out and that we should come get any valuables. My mother took me with her to the apartment to clean it out. I have often wondered why. Maybe because it was once my home too. Maybe she thought I needed to see it. Or maybe she just needed assistance and was too embarrassed to ask one of her girlfriends or siblings. Whatever the reason, it was devastating to see the condition of my childhood home. Our dog, Fever, had been abandoned in that house with my sister and her strung-out crew and had died of malnutrition. The smell of urine and dog feces and crack, which smells like what I imagine the bowels of hell smell like, consumed the apartment. I wanted to run out as soon as we entered, but I followed my mom inside, and at some point during the visit I used the bathroom. My mom was so irritated with me for going to the bathroom in that apartment that we left shortly after, and a day or so later the itching started.

My mother and my grandmother took me to that appointment and sat with me in the exam room. The doctor did all the regular things, like pressing on my tummy and listening to my heart. He only made me take off my pants and then moved my underwear to the side to take a quick look and swab from my vagina. I was dressed almost as quickly as I was undressed, and then I sat in the waiting area with my grandma while my mother and the doctor talked. Our apartment was right down the street. We left the clinic and my mother didn't say a single thing to me, but she was filling my grandmother in on her conversation with the doctor. When we crossed the big intersection by our building, my mother stopped on the corner and turned to me.

"You know you are going to have to give them a list of all of the people you have had sex with if you have a sexually transmitted disease, right?"

I froze.

"The doctors will have to call them all and let them know!"

She was disgusted with me. It was all in her voice. I stared at her in silence, but my eyes must have delivered something that my mouth couldn't carry because she followed with, "Don't look at me like that—this is on you!"

I took a quick glance over her shoulder at my grandmother, maybe hoping for some reprieve, but she didn't say a word. We started walking again and they continued with their conversation as the world swirled around me. I slowed my steps so that I could fix my face before I had to hear it from my mother. I did everything in my power not to cry. We got to the house and I went into my room. I sat on my bed, feeling dizzy and confused while replaying my mother's admonishment. *Sex partners*? Did she think I was having sex with boys? Of my own free will? Did I have a sexually transmitted disease? I had so many questions, but I kept coming back to one: Why did she hate me?

It felt like she was always angry at me for one reason or another. I had grown more accustomed to it, especially since Mr. Eddie had come into our lives. But what must she think of me to believe I was a *whore* at twelve without considering that I might be a victim? I was too young and scared to ask that question. As I got older I heard stories of women who resented their children or mistreated them because they looked just like their fathers—the ones who had abandoned the family or mistreated the mothers. I am, however, my mother's spitting image. People often look at photos of us both as young girls and can't tell us apart. I don't know much about my biological father, but I know that the circumstances of my birth are painful to my mother. In later years, I've thought that it was maybe not hate she had for me, but for herself. Maybe what I felt from her as a child was a manifestation of the pain and memories that my reflection brought up in her.

There is no question that self-hate severely limits one's capacity to love fully and wholeheartedly. Capacity and desire are not the same thing, especially in discussions of love. I was an adult with a child of my own and a trail of mistakes behind me before I could say with certainty that my mother loved me. That clarity came from being faced with my own limited capacity. No matter how deep my desire was to love my child, I was still encumbered by the ghosts I had tried to bury. I failed—often. If I hadn't had the experiences I had with my mother, I'm not sure I would have fought so hard to build my capacity. Resting on my desire was not enough to both love and liberate my child in the way I wanted to. Like so many women raising children who were brought into the world on purpose, and also maybe to serve multiple purposes—to glue together a relationship, to be a personal source of love and adoration, or a proof of worth—I know how hard it hits when you realize that each life has its own purpose, even the lives of our children, and that purpose is not dictated by our needs.

After that day we never discussed the doctor's visit, just like we would never discuss the ob-gyn visit that came later. I just assumed it wasn't an STD because we didn't have a follow-up and I wasn't asked to provide any list. That night, Mr. Eddie had me soak in what he called a sitz bath. He put a pail in the tub and added warm water, goldenseal, black seed oil, and some other natural products and told me to sit in it until he knocked on the door. I did the sitz bath at least two more times, and about a week later the rash cleared up.

"You have to be careful where you go to the bathroom and how you wipe yourself, okay?" he told me. "You're a young lady, so you have to be careful."

This was how his niceness showed up—sporadically but somehow magically on time. He never asked me what happened or how it happened, and I wasn't sure that I would even tell if I was asked directly. That moment on the street corner with my mother and grandmother felt like my one and only opportunity to get it out, and before it could even become a real chance, it was gone.

brand new day

Before I was a senior, I had my heart set on attending Clark Atlanta University in Georgia. We had stopped at the campus on the way home from a 21st Century Youth Leadership trip and ran right into a group of student organizers in the parking lot. They talked to us about the school and how much they loved it as well as challenges they felt as students. After high school, I wanted to go somewhere I could find like-minded people, continue organizing for my community, and also grow intellectually. After talking to the

Atlanta student activists, I wanted to go there *badly*. I didn't know much about HBCUs (Historically Black Colleges and Universities) beyond Spike Lee's *School Daze* and *A Different World*, which was kind of enough. But that, combined with my experience at the Atlanta University Complex—better known as the AUC, which housed Spelman, Morehouse, and Morris Brown colleges, as well as Clark Atlanta University— sealed it for me. When I got in that spring I was ecstatic, but my euphoria quickly faded when I found out that my financial aid wasn't going to be enough to cover tuition.

My mother had gone to college in the city. It was completely paid for by financial aid, so she could not comprehend why I needed to go away to school when I could stay in New York and basically go for free. Securing financial aid beyond what the federal and state governments provided was also foreign to her. Despite me being in honors and Regents classes, having great grades, a pretty decent SAT score, and a mother, grandmother, and others in my family who attended college, my guidance counselor believed it would be best for me to attend Bronx Community College to "test the waters." She didn't help me with the application fee waivers for any of the colleges I applied to, so she certainly wasn't going to help me figure out financial aid once I was accepted. I just had to figure it out. I was smart and capable and tried to make rational, sound decisions, but I was only seventeen. I decided I would work for a semester, save up, and go to Clark Atlanta University in the spring.

I was at my job with the New York chapter of 21st Century located at Jobs for Youth, our sponsoring organization, when I got a call from Mrs. Sanders. She called pretty regularly to check in on our progress and assign us various books to read or activities to complete that helped build our skills, so I wasn't surprised when I picked up the phone and heard her voice. It was late August. She started by asking me where I had decided to go in the fall. I told her that I was sitting out for a semester, explaining my financial situation and detailing my plan to go to Atlanta in the spring.

There was a moment of silence on the other end before I heard her exhale.

"Tawana"—that was her nickname for me—"everyone I know who sits out finds a reason not to go back. Do you trust me?"

I laughed. No adult had ever asked me that before.

"Yes, I trust you," I answered, but my heart quickened. I had become accustomed to not trusting anyone outside of my family. I knew my family would always come through for me in one way or another. My granddaddy had assured me of that. I knew that I had good adults around me in school and in extracurricular activities, but I didn't have any expectation that they would go out of their way for me. Then there was Mrs. Sanders. She was larger than life to me. She was an alchemist, a dream weaver, a warrior. She had crafted a universe for us to evolve and thrive and shape-shift into believers in our own infinite and immediate power—the leaders she was sure we already were. Of course I trusted her.

She proceeded to explain that she could get me into Alabama State University. She told me a bit about it and said that if I trusted her, she would call me back with more information. I did—and she did. She asked me to fax over a copy of my high school diploma to the admissions office and then call and ask for a specific woman. I told her I needed to collect everything, but that I would call the next day.

I went home that night and didn't tell my mother about Mrs. Sanders's phone call. She had not really asked me what my plans were once it became clear that Clark Atlanta wasn't going to happen that fall. I hadn't even told her about my plan to save and go later. In fact, we didn't really talk at all anymore. I had been going to school every day, following the rules she put down (generally), and living a life in which my mother was only tangentially involved. Graduation came and went. I talked about attending Lehman College or maybe Bronx Community, but made no active plans. All my mom knew was that I had a job for the summer. When I was home, I felt alone. When it came to this new opportunity, I didn't want to be set upon with a thousand questions that I didn't know how to answer, including who was going to pay for it. I didn't know what was going to come next, and it didn't help that the plan was completely unorthodox. So I just kept quiet. I went back to work the next day with my diploma and followed Mrs. Sanders's instructions step by step.

I picked up the office phone, punched in the number she gave me, and asked for the woman. She spoke with none of Mrs. Sanders's warmth, asking me short, clipped questions.

"Who told you to call me?"

She asked with a thick Southern drawl and a serious attitude, as if I were disturbing her during her soaps.

"Rose Sanders. Attorney Rose Sanders, from Selma."

I felt shaky as hell. I had no idea what I was getting into or if this was going to work. But when I answered, her tone immediately shifted.

"Ohhhhhh, Mrs. SANDERS! Yes! Okay, baby . . . did you fax me your diploma?"

The clipped edge to her voice was gone. In its place was a startling effusiveness.

"Yes, I did, just a few minutes ago."

She put me on hold for a minute before coming back to say she needed a few more things. I gave her my address, social security number, date of birth, and a few other bits of personal information. She told me to get a pen and then rattled off some names and numbers to call after I got off the phone with her.

"You gon' hafta call to the financial aid and speak to them 'bout your FAFSA. You have that, right?"

"Yes, I have it."

"Okay, good. And you gon' hafta call over to housing to see what they can do because you know folks already in the dorms and got they assignments."

"Oh, okay."

"Okay, I'm 'bout to fax you a letter and some paperwork that you gon' hafta to send right back to me. Can you do that?"

"Yes, I can do that. I'm right by the fax machine."

"Okay, hold on to that letter because you gon' need that when you making these other calls. But send me the other papers right back after you fill them out, okay? Don't worry about the last question on the second page—just get me the rest as soon as you can."

"Okay, I will. Thank you."

I hung up the phone absolutely confused. I had listened to her intently and had taken down all the names and numbers, but I didn't know what any of it meant. The fax machine started ringing in the middle of my perplexia, and my confusion quickly turned to disbelief. A letter came through that opened with the following sentence: *Congratulations on being admitted to Alabama State University*. The second set of papers that came through had bold words printed at the top of the first page: APPLICATION FOR ADMISSION.

It was clearly a major come up. I don't know who Mrs. Sanders had called or what strings she pulled to get me into that school, but it was on paper and official. Just twenty-four hours after I decided to trust her and take a chance, I was enrolled in college. I spent the rest of the afternoon making the other phone calls and faxing the additional paperwork. I laid out all the information in a notebook and went home to face my mother. I was too excited to worry about how to do it just right, and the whole story tumbled out of me as soon as I got in the house. When I was done, she just stared at me.

"Just like that?" she started.

"Yup, just like that." I tried not to sound too enthusiastic.

"So you're supposed to pick up and go off to college in Alabama when?"

"They said I need to get there by next week so I can keep my room. Mrs. Sanders paid the deposit to hold it already."

"And what about books and supplies and all of that kind of stuff?"

"Mrs. Sanders said don't worry about all of that now, just get there."

"Mrs. Sanders said, huh."

I waited for the bomb to drop. There was always a bomb with my mother. I tried to dampen my excitement so as not to stir her up. My mother, without spending a single dollar, and maybe unbeknownst to her, had gifted me with so much, but her greatest gift was knowing when I most needed her to say yes. She said yes to letting me read books and try new activities and go on trips like the one where I discovered 21C. The older I got, the more each yes gave way to bigger and better opportunities, but the yeses also seemed more difficult to come by and were matched with what felt like increasing resentment. I wouldn't have been able to appreciate the doors Mrs. Sanders had opened for me without the groundwork my mother had laid and the importance she had placed on education and culture, but she sometimes made walking through those doors feel like walking through a minefield. Now I had gotten everything that might involve her doing something extra or spending money covered, except one thing.

"So how are you going to get there?" She looked me directly in the eyes, like she had finally caught me.

"I . . . I need you to get me a ticket," I stammered. *Damn*, I thought. I didn't want to let her see me sweat.

The truth was that Mrs. Sanders had already offered to get me a plane ticket. I told her that my mother would take care of that—because I thought she should. Now regret crept in. Although I never had too many details about our financial situation, I knew that money was perpetually tight and I tried not to ask for things that were outlandish or selfish.

"With what money, *Tarana Janeen*?"

As soon as I heard both my names I knew that I had tripped a wire.

She only ever used my first and middle name when she was agitated.

"I'm supposed to just find money for you to fly to Alabama, just like that, because you decided to pick up and go away?" And then she started chuckling, but not because she was amused. It was more of a *hmph* mixed with *yeah right*. I stayed quiet. I knew to just let this play out.

"Okay, Tarana," she said, shaking her head and sighing. "We'll see. I'm not making promises because I was not budgeting for this."

I left quickly and disappeared into my room. Hot tears came. *Why is she like this?* It felt as if she enjoyed keeping me in limbo. Like she got some power out of knowing I was hanging in the balance, knowing I was waiting for her approval or denial. Didn't she want me to go to college? Wasn't she glad I had found a way to go with minimal cost to her? *How is she not just happy for me? Why can't she just be fucking proud of me once?* I cried until sleep took me. The next morning I prepared myself to swallow my pride and let Mrs. Sanders know that I would need her to buy my ticket after all.

When I woke up, my brother's father, Mr. Eddie, was at the house. By the time I was a senior in high school, Mr.

Eddie had not lived with us for years but he still came and went as he pleased. He greeted me with a rare smile and an even rarer hug and kiss.

"I hear congratulations are in order," he said in his deep, slick voice. This was one of those times when he and my mom were "on," and he was over pretty regularly. I still didn't like him, but mostly for my mother, who I thought deserved someone who prioritized her. But him being gone had been good for my relationship with him. He wasn't in my face all the time and had chilled out since I had gotten older.

"What are you talking about?" I said, still rubbing sleep out of my eyes.

He responded with his signature thunderous laugh, which jolted me fully awake.

"Your mammy said you are going off to COLLEGE!"

I half smiled at him, trying to understand why he was so enthusiastic.

"Why the long face?" he asked. "Aren't you happy to be going off to *COLLEGE*!"

Every time he said the word "college," he emphasized it like he was saying a million *DOLLARS*! It was all very weird. I managed to tell him that I was excited at the opportunity to go to Alabama State, but I still had to see what was going to happen.

"See what's gonna happen?!" He seemed incredulous, something he rarely was. "Ya mammy said all you needed was a plane ticket. What else you need?"

Then it clicked. My mom had done that thing she did where she'd show me no enthusiasm, then would go and brag to him about it. It had always made me feel like a pawn in their weird game, but now I couldn't help tentatively smiling, knowing my mom had bragged about this.

"That's it, I guess," I said. "A plane ticket."

"Oh, well, that's nothing. I got that," he was all too anxious to inform me. "Please! What else you need? Clothes, books, new pair of shoes? What?"

I studied his face with caution and curiosity. Our relationship had evolved some, but not this much. I had seen him bait and switch my mom like this with fake excitement that he'd turn off just as she joined him in it. This did seem different, though. His enthusiasm was weird, but increasingly infectious. Finally, unable to hold it in any longer, I laughed out loud at how jumpy and jubilant this moment was making him.

"I don't know," I giggled. "This all happened yesterday!"

By now my mother had come into the room. Her demeanor was decidedly different from the day before. She started talking to both of us about what she was going to run out and get from the store that day—things like toiletries and supplies. Then she told me to call the school and see if they had a list of stuff I should bring. I didn't know what had happened between me going to bed and waking up, but I didn't care. This was happening.

In less than a week, I was set and ready to go. It was the first time I had ever been on a plane, but that part felt insignificant in comparison to the bigger adventure of college. My whole focus was on this new beginning. Everything I had was riding on this next chapter. No one knew me. No one knew my secrets. It was yet another chance at reinvention. Whoever I was when I stepped onto that campus was who I would be for the rest of my life, and I was dying to find out who that person was. In keeping my secrets I had inadvertently trapped some of the best parts of myself. I wanted so desperately to be free—to lean into the life I kept getting glimpses of.

sweet home alabama

I was still seventeen when I packed up and went to college. I had no trepidation about being away from home. I thought that because I had traveled to Selma and other places the past few years, I knew how to handle standing out because of clothes or music taste. Then I arrived.

Nothing I experienced in 21C had prepared me for life at an HBCU in the Deep South. I was no longer surrounded by young, hopeful leaders looking to uplift their communities. I was living in a Luke video set inside a subwoofer. Every car that passed was playing bass music so loud it felt like we were permanently living on a washing machine in spin cycle. The guys wore biking shorts—intentionally. The girls were still wearing stacks in their hair from four Salt-N-Pepa videos ago, with baby hairs gelled into adolescence across their foreheads. I was two weeks late in arriving, and bonds and cliques were already starting to form. So I walked around for the first week silently, both in and out of class. Instead of making friends, I roamed the yard wearing my Walkman and listening to Kid Capri mixtapes that reminded me of home.

The first kid I met was named Fred. I was sitting in front of the dorm when yet another lowrider came pulling through the yard blasting "Drop" by DJ Magic Mike, a bass-heavy anthem that made guys and girls alike bounce and shake. As soon as I saw the car starting up the road, I got up and put on my Walkman. I had just pressed play when a hand touched my shoulder. I jumped and spun around, ready to fight. When I looked to see who had touched me, there was a six-foot-something, light-skinned dude with a fade and a lot of face. His whole vibe was straight out of *The Fresh Prince of Bel-Air*.

"My bad, dawg, I ain't mean to scare you!" He was laughing and holding his hand back, ready to give me five from the side like Will gave Jazz on the show. I looked at him, then at his hand, then back at him without ever turning my music off or dropping my scowl.

"Daaaaaaaaaaaaaaang!" He let the vowel sit on his tongue for a long time, while covering his mouth with his fist. I pulled one headphone off my ear, trying to figure out why he was still in my face.

"Dang, what?" I deadpanned. "Is there a problem?"

I was still scowling, but I was also intrigued that he hadn't dismissed me like so many other students had. This dude was unmoved. In fact, he was amused.

"New York, right? You gotta be from New York!" He didn't even wait for my response. "Oh, I'm Fred, but everyone calls me Boston because—guess why?" He pointed at me with a big, silly, open-mouth grin as if queuing me to fill in the blank.

"Cuz you from Philly," I threw back at him, and he cracked up laughing. His laughter was from his gut. It was loud and infectious, and it took less than thirty seconds before I was caught up in it and laughing too. I confirmed that I was from New York and that I didn't see myself staying at the school for much longer if the music persisted and people kept asking me stupid questions. Boston assured me that I had not been introduced to the right folks yet, then appointed himself my one-man college concierge service.

His first order of business was to introduce me to all the kids from "up top," or the East Coast. This Deep South college campus had managed to do something that I never saw at home. In this new place, far from the shadow of the bridge and tunnel, being from Jersey was just as cool as being from the boroughs of New York, Queens and the Bronx had no qualms, and even places like Connecticut and Delaware were thrown into the mix.

I was quickly inducted into the up top clique. A smaller group of cool-ass girls I'd connected with in my dorm split off as my everyday crew. They were from all over the place. My roommate from Chicago and her bestie from Jersey were more loosely associated, but my three main girlfriends were two high school friends from Atlanta and one girl from Queens. There were also some cool guys. Boston, who was kind of in everybody's crew; a dude from Poughkeepsie who we called Kip for short; Big W, a ginormous six-five, light-skinned house-head with locs; O, who was goofy and lovable but scary strong; and Rob, a deliciously dark-skinned dred from Harlem, with thick lips that gave away his penchant for blunts and a voice so deep and uptown that he spoke in a growl. I was crushing hard on Rob and would delight in watching him move across campus, slow and deliberate, dapping random people and giving shout-outs with a chew stick hanging from the side of his mouth. I was still dating Sean, my high school boyfriend, and one of the girls in the crew was wide open off of Rob, so I never said a thing. But I took every opportunity to hang out with him.

Going to parties and events in mixed groups, which we rarely did at home, was commonplace in college. The social rules I was used to didn't apply. I was at a party with my new friends when I saw a guy across the room wearing loosely tied Timbs—too loose, which was a dead giveaway that he was corny—and a starter jersey. I tried to be nice and cheery.

"Hey, what's up? You from New York?" I said, throwing in a smile.

He whipped his head around so fast I was forced to take a small step back.

"You talking to me?!" He was both questioning and nasty. Before I could respond, he turned his whole body to face me and stomped a Timb directly in front of my feet, announcing loudly to the room, "Mount Vernon, *WHAT*?"

I could tell the dudes around him were impressed by this fake swag. I could also tell this guy was a fraud who had taken college as an opportunity to reinvent himself, even though he probably got chased home every day on his block.

My mouth opened before my brain could stop it. "Nigga, unless you the overweight lover Heavy D or Al B. Sure, nobody gives a *fuck* about Mount Vernon. Nigga, I'm from the Bronx. You don't want to cross this street!"

I was on a roll. No one but he and I knew what I was talking about, but it didn't matter. We had a crowd now, and he was trying desperately to backtrack.

"Ooooh, you from BX! Oooooh! Yeah, Boogie Down in the house!"

He was trying to hype me up, which made me even more irritated, but eventually he calmed the bravado and I backed down because it felt like things were cool. I stepped back and turned to leave and he yelled out, "Imma call you Boogie Down Productions!" He burst into laughter along with his boys.

I stopped dead in my tracks. Ever since seventh grade, when the hip-hop group BDP, or Boogie Down Productions, led by the legendary MC KRS-One, came out, I had been dogged by comparisons to KRS-One. The first time I ever heard it was when a girl in my eighth grade class casually turned around and said, "You know you look like KRS-One?" She snickered and turned back around satisfied with herself. I actually loved the group, but I had no idea what KRS looked like, and the way she said it made it sound like an insult. The comparison came up again in high school, when I'd started dating Sean. One of his friends would sing random BDP songs whenever he saw us together until my boyfriend checked him.

It always seemed like a weird diss to me, though. We both have big, broad, African noses and full lips. I was raised to love everything African and everything that made me more African, like my nose. My granddaddy would always point out, with disdain, how lighter-skinned folks were too close to white and how we were lucky to still be identifiably African. And I loved Kris Parker, or KRS. He was one of my all-time favorite rappers and personal heroes as a kid. None of that mattered, though. I was a dark-skinned, loud-mouthed Black girl, and how dare I be visible and opinionated or anything that rubbed up against what white folks told my folks was acceptable. These insults were meant to force me back into my place. It was the cleaner, nicer version of *"You got a lotta mouth for an ugly bitch."*

I stood there, initially expecting to be thrown right back to my old injuries, but then remembering I had a mission. I didn't want to be tripped up by the first dusty dude with old, wack insults. This cornball wasn't the only one who had decided to reinvent himself in this new place. I knew and respected Mount Vernon dudes. It wasn't where he was from. Every bone in my body knew he was a "herb." I could probably end his college career by taking it straight to his chin.

Instead I screamed back, "Call me whatever the fuck you want, nigga, as long as you know I'm still Number One!" It was a reference to one of BDP's most famous songs, and it was probably lost on some of the people around us but not on him, and not on my newfound crew, who were putting batteries in my back the whole time. When he saw me on the yard after that, it was always head nods and pounds. I had stared down one of my demons and won.

※

Finding my tribe on campus opened everything up for me. One night, the crew was hanging out on the lawn, shooting the shit. It came up that I'd never had a drink before, and Rob was the first to speak up.

"Ooh, we 'bout to change that!"

I may have had an attitude and a quick temper, but in high school I'd been a good kid as far as not sneaking out and getting drunk or partying. I had tried weed in the ninth grade, and after a ten-minute coughing fit I fell asleep. I didn't like the idea of not having all my faculties. I always wanted to have my wits about me in case something popped off. In college I could be the life of the party without getting drunk, and often people didn't realize that I hadn't been drinking.

I looked at Rob, my eyes settling on the smirk that had spread across his thick lips.

"I'ont know about that, y'all." Another guy had produced a big brown bag and I casually looked in to see a couple of bottles of liquor. I pulled one out randomly and read it out loud. "M-D-20-20 . . . What is this? It looks like Kool-Aid in a liquor bottle!"

The whole crew laughed.

"You never heard of that, mad dog?" someone asked.

"Nah," I told them. "But it looks like some wino shit."

Then Rob took the bottle and looked right at me. "Well, this is where we'll start, then."

He cracked open the bottle and handed it to me as he guzzled his Heineken. I took a quick, full swig and nearly choked. The sharp taste of a melted grape Jolly Rancher mixed with rubbing alcohol hit the back of my throat. Everyone laughed at how green I was and insisted I keep going. I took two or three more full swallows, letting the saccharine acid settle in my stomach. One moment I was sitting on the steps and the next I was hearing my own voice booming, but I didn't remember starting to talk. I was yelling now, but I felt like I was watching myself, coming in and out of the real world. The rest of the night happened in snippets: disrupting a basketball game by attempting to sit with the coach on his lap, sparking arguments with onlookers who stared a second too long, challenging my friends to races around the yard, and singing and rapping at the top of my lungs. The night ended with turned stomachs and tossed cookies for some, but for me it was crash sleeping in my clothes and waking the next day feeling like someone had drop-kicked me across campus. I panicked, remembering stories of girls being taken advantage of while drunk with their guy friends. We gathered later that day to swap tales and laugh at the previous evening's shenanigans. I learned two things: that I could go from a happy to a mean drunk in a second and that I was safe with this crew.

My crush on Rob only grew after that night, but I was determined to be faithful to my boyfriend at home and respect my friend who talked about him nonstop. The only time I let myself go was on the dance floor. I'd never had the chance to really let loose in high school. My boyfriend was jealous and controlling, and my mom didn't really let me go to parties, but I still loved to dance and would practice in my room. Rob and I had something of a thing when we were at a party and the music switched to dancehall. Rob didn't have Caribbean roots like me, but he was New York enough, and he brought his authentic energy to the dance floor. They never played the music for long, maybe two songs, but whenever they did we found each other and let out whatever pent-up sexual energy we were both trying to ignore. We danced like no one else was there, like it was a mating ritual and we had fire in our bellies. I loved every minute of it. It was the first time in my life that I got to safely explore my sexuality with no demands on my body. I danced with him like he was my lover, but we left it on the dance floor. We never so much as kissed that whole year. I even helped facilitate a late-night meetup between him and the girl who was so in love with him, joking that if she didn't make her move I would.

I was completely settled in at State in no time. I went to classes and hung out with my friends most evenings that I wasn't studying. I started dreaming about things like pledging a sorority, which had never crossed my mind before, and I joined a student organization called DOMA (Descendants of Mother Africa). Back home, my love life had imploded, but this crew made life bearable and made me feel good.

At the start of my second semester, Sean told me he had gotten another girl pregnant. I was devastated. I had been so faithful to him that girls in my dorm would come find me when he called on the hallway pay phone. I had made a decision when we first slept together: if he was the first, he would also be the last. That was the only way I could finally move on from what had happened to me. We had daydreamed about a life together, and in my mind he had thrown it away. What was I being faithful for? I had done all the things I was supposed to do, including staying away from Rob, and still he betrayed me. I stopped going to classes regularly, staying in my room for weeks, until more than midway through the semester. That was when the verdict came in from the Rodney King trial.

In the spring of 1991, when I was a senior in high school and cell phones didn't have cameras and were only used by drug dealers and car salesmen, a man named Rodney King was almost beaten to death by police officers in Los Angeles during a routine DUI arrest. The beating would have been spun by police as a case of resisting arrest, but a man nearby with a camcorder caught it all on video and sent it to the local news station. Soon it was on every station in the country and world. The incident put racial profiling and police brutality front and center in the media. As an organizer in New York, I had already been wrapped up in the murders of Yusef Hawkins and the Central Park Jogger case. Rodney King happened in LA, but the footage made it feel like our backyard. Not too long before King's assault, a fifteen-year-old Black girl named Latasha Harlins was murdered by a fifty-one-year-old Korean convenience-store owner in Los Angeles who accused Latasha of stealing. During my first semester at Alabama State, the store owner was found guilty of voluntary manslaughter, but the judge threw out the recommendation of sixteen years and instead gave a sentence that called for no jail time. Now, in the spring of 1992, the four officers charged with attempting to murder Rodney King with excessive force were acquitted. All four of them were freed. The city of Los Angeles exploded, and the people took to the streets in an uprising unlike anything America had seen since the '60s. The eruption was felt across the country.

I heard the verdict while still moping in my room. I had taken up lying around listening to sad, slow jams, but this news jolted me out of bed. I got dressed and ran downstairs to try to find out what was happening on campus. No one was hanging in the lobby of the dorm, and when I walked out onto the yard it was all business as usual. Everyone I stopped and asked about Rodney King had no idea what I was talking about. They were even dismissive of my growing rage.

After walking the yard, I went to the library and hand-wrote a flyer: IF YOU ARE ANGRY ABOUT RODNEY KING AND LATASHA HARLINS, MEET ME IN FRONT OF THE MAIN DINING HALL TOMORROW AT 12PM. Then I went to visit with one of my favorite office ladies in the admissions building and asked her to make a few copies. She made them but told me if I didn't have them stamped by the dean's office, then they would just pull them down. I marched to the dean's office, where I got a song and dance about preapproval and paperwork. I took my fliers and headed back to the dorm, remembering one of my elders' advice: "Sometimes it's better to apologize than to wait for permission."

Back in my dorm room, I thought hard about how I could organize a protest on campus that wouldn't get shut down. I looked at my reflection in my mirror. I was wearing a big black headwrap and giant hoop earrings, one of my signature looks. It was made of about two yards of jersey cotton that I could wrap two feet high on top of my head. As I studied myself, suddenly I had the answer. I pulled the headwrap off and took out my scissors, carefully folding and cutting it into as many strips as I could. I took the strips and my fliers and went back outside to look for my crew.

We headed to the main dining hall. It was the most popular spot on the yard in the middle of the day and it was bustling with activity. I went to the top of the steps and, using my voice as a bullhorn, began to talk about the rally. One of my friends passed out the fliers, another the black fabric strips. It felt reminiscent of my days in my 21C chapter, and the adrenaline made my heart race. I was suddenly too hyped to be sad. I implored my fellow students to make their voices heard and wear the black cloth tied around their right arms in a show of solidarity. Lots of kids willfully ignored us, but a crowd eventually started to form. Kids were taking the material and reading the flier. Others just called out support.

When I came down off the steps, there were two older students waiting. They told me that the student body president wanted to talk to me. I didn't know him personally—I was a freshman and he was an upperclassman—but I knew he was a "Que," or a member of Omega Psi Phi fraternity. Girls swooned every time his name came up and *everyone* seemed to like him.

The two older students ushered me to his office. He was wearing a suit and looked like a young administrator. He greeted us with a big smile, then told me that "we had a problem." He said that the president of the college was aware of the outrage that we all felt and was behind us, as was the Student Government Association (SGA), but they wanted to make sure it was done the "right way." His voice was cool as he said that because my event wasn't sanctioned, the school would shut it down. I told him I didn't care because protests didn't have to be sanctioned.

"Besides, if they shut it down, it would be all over the news."

He looked surprised. "You called the media?"

"Yup," I lied. "And I have Rose Sanders coming to speak."

I knew that Mrs. Sanders's name held some weight on campus, or at least caused people to sit up and listen. He adjusted quickly, suggesting we coordinate. He was planning something anyway, he revealed. We talked some more about the logistics, and I left feeling a surge of energy. I loved organizing. I loved being productive. And now I had to get Mrs. Sanders on board because I didn't love being embarrassed. I called her at the law office and explained that I had already told them she would come speak.

I heard her familiar chuckle through the phone.

"Honey, Joe"—referring to Joe Reed, a prominent member of the school's board of trustees—"already called me. I told him you'd speak."

My whole body turned to pins and needles, and before I knew what I was doing, I screamed into the phone, "I CAN'T, MRS. SANDERS!"

"Why can't you? You wanted this, now go ahead and do it. Besides, if you don't those fools up in Montgomery will take over, so we need some 21st Century Leaders to stand their ground."

In a daze, I agreed and hung up. I knew how to lead a rally. I could get the students hyped up but I didn't know how to make a speech, or at least I had only done it a couple of times before. Excitement and fear mixed in my stomach. I knew I had to show up ready.

The SGA pulled out all the stops for what was now a press event. They actually organized the press and lined up speakers and had sound systems and podiums and everything covered. As much as I wanted to feel like they stole my idea and event, what they organized in short order was more than I could do with my homemade fliers and cut-up headwrap. It still felt stuffy to me, but it was a lesson in how collaboration and preparation are just as important as passion.

The speakers came and went quickly, the adult admins mostly encouraging students not to riot or react like the folks in LA. Then, the SGA president came up and gave a measured but passionate speech that gave the crowd a bit more energy. I stood on the steps, watching and waiting my turn. When he finished and motioned for me to come to the mic, the only thing I could hear was the roar of my crew screaming and calling my name. I moved up the steps, my nerves getting worse with each step. I am not a natural public speaker. Like many, I hate the sound of my voice. Being in Alabama made me even more self-conscious, because my Bronx accent stood out amid the twang of my Alabama homies. I felt like people only heard a hood rat when I spoke. But those thoughts fell away as I stepped in front of the mic—I was fired up.

"I've heard a lot of things today, but one thing I haven't heard is the name Latasha Harlins," I began. As soon as I said her name, the crowd erupted into cheers, chanting her name. I did my best to channel Rose Sanders. My fears about being able to make a speech went away as the few bullet points I had jotted down morphed into an impassioned plea for my fellow students to get active and stay active. I did what I did best: rallied my folks.

I stepped away from the podium with a fire lit inside me. I forgot about cheating boyfriends and missed classes. The school year was nearly over, but I had finally found my footing. I had been entertaining thoughts of not returning the following year, but those were gone now. I felt powerful. I had set out to reinvent myself, but it turned out that I didn't have to start from scratch. I just had to dust myself off, because the best parts were already there.

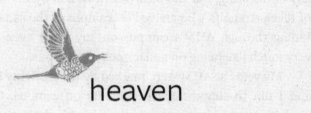

heaven

As hard as it was to be far away from home and not have the same kind of resources as other students, I made a way. When I returned to Alabama State for my sophomore year, half of my crew was gone. Some of my closest girlfriends didn't come back; Rob transferred to a school back in New York. I had also changed, and by my junior year there was so much turmoil in the administration that it was hard to focus on just being a student. Our new university president made sweeping changes that made it obvious he did not put students first. One of those changes was that students who depended on financial aid were required pay their tuition up front and be reimbursed when federal aid came through. With the number of students attending the school from low-wealth communities, there was no way for us to attend with that kind of policy. We protested and fought back, and eventually a number of policies were rescinded, but the damage had been done. I made the hard decision to join the mass exodus from ASU and transfer to Auburn University at Montgomery. Moving from an HBCU to a PWI (Predominately White Institution) can be culturally devastating, but the blow was lessened by the number of Black students who arrived on campus at the same time. Riding through AUM's campus on any given evening felt very much like being on a Black college campus.

My years at AUM were marked by the work my friends and I did to support Black students on campus. One of my best friends from 21C, Eddie, who I had convinced to come to Alabama State my sophomore year, transferred to AUM with me. We formed a new crew along with our friend Perry Varner. Perry knew everyone in Montgomery, and he introduced us like we were old friends or family. The administration was not prepared for this new wave of Black kids on campus. Eddie, Perry, and I created the African American Student Alliance, which became the organization that brought Black students together across various affiliations. It didn't matter what fraternity or sorority you had pledged or who you were aligned with socially: AASA was Switzerland, and because of that we got a lot of work done.

By the time I was a senior, I thought I was clear on what my future held: nonprofit administration. Because I was in

Alabama, I stayed very active with the 21st Century Youth Leadership Movement the entire time I was in college. I moved up, even becoming a board member. I saw the inner workings of the organization and learned about fundraising and how we kept the doors open. I had decided that I was going to work for a big foundation like Ford or Rockefeller when I graduated. I wanted to be a movement person with real, firsthand knowledge of what it took to run an organization that was helping to move money out into the field. I wanted to make it so organizations like 21C no longer had to beg for financial support. I proudly announced these plans at one of our board meetings. After my short speech, Senator Sanders, Mrs. Sanders's husband and 21C cofounder, leaned forward in his chair and looked right at me.

"That sounds lovely, Tarana, it really does, and I appreciate hearing that kind of passion from young folk, but what if I made you a different offer?"

He had never really addressed me directly before, and I didn't know what to say. I let out a nervous laugh. "Okay, like what?"

He continued, looking only at me. "What if you moved to Selma and worked for 21st Century?"

Record scratch. My mouth fell open as he went on.

"We need a resource development person who will focus on fundraising for the organization. That work seems to excite you, and we already know that you love 21st Century and are excited to be a 21st Century Leader. It feels like a good fit."

I was stunned. I had been making plans to move back to New York or Maryland with Sean. We were "on" again despite everything, and things felt solid. Now this new opportunity was presented and it hit all the right notes. I would not have to search for a job; I would be doing work that I felt passionate about for an organization I loved and trusted. I didn't quite trust a life with this boyfriend or back in New York. This was a real opportunity with real substance. It felt like the smart thing to do, and so I accepted.

They didn't hire only me right out of college. They also hired Malika Sanders, the oldest of the Sanders's three children and a recent college graduate, who I had grown up with in the organization, and LaTosha Brown, a local youth leader in Selma, who didn't come up in 21C but who I had attended AUM with.

When most people think of Selma, they think of old documentary footage of marchers being beaten on Bloody Sunday or the racist sheriff, Jim Clark, shoving Annie Cooper to the ground for trying to register to vote. Every year thousands participate or watch the annual trek across the Edmund Pettus Bridge to commemorate the historic events. But Selma after the movement was in many ways the same as Selma before. It was poor. Black people were overpoliced and underserved, and the violence of plantation slavery lived on in ways that were both obvious and hidden. Malika, LaTosha, and I were charged with bringing the organization, and the movement in Selma, into the twenty-first century. I had no idea at the time how difficult that would be.

Like everything else at 21C—and at most small, grassroots organizations—job titles didn't actually mean just doing *that* job. Although I was hired to raise money, it quickly became clear that I would also work on whatever else was needed—including my favorite part of the organization, the camps. Leadership camp was at the heart of 21C work.

In 1996, the year I started working at 21C, we had more than forty chapters across the South, in major cities like New York, Boston, and Chicago, and an international chapter in Mali. Each chapter was autonomous, but three times annually all the chapters gathered for training and community building. These were our camps. There were short, three-day events in the spring and winter, each on a different HBCU campus, and then a longer, ten-day camp in the summer in Selma. As a youth member, I had missed camp only twice since I started in 1989: once in December 1990, when I was on punishment and my mother refused to let me go to a winter camp at Tuskegee, and again in 1994, when the New York chapter decided—against my very loud protest—to host their own summer camp in New York. The new leadership at the time didn't understand that traveling for the camps, especially the summer camp, was a part of the whole experience. A lot of chapters couldn't afford to get their members to the weekend camps, so most saved their resources for summer. It was too important to miss. It was what endeared and committed me to the organization. It was also where I met my chosen family. We laughed, cried, sang, danced, testified, chanted, organized, learned, taught, and loved for ten days straight. For a lot of us, it was more love than we had ever received—or given. It was a sacred space. People came with trauma, and while dealing with trauma wasn't an official part of the 21C agenda, it existed in so many of us that dealing with it was inevitable. The organization centered the needs, experiences, and futures of

Black and Brown youth, and many of us arrived with gaping wounds from a variety of tragedies in our homes and home-towns. I was no different. I just didn't realize it yet.

I felt a deep sense of community as a youth camp leader. I was able to build on my skills as a leader and come back to my community invigorated to effect change. As an employee of the organization, I wanted to make sure that we created space for the next wave of young people to experience the same things.

In the summer of 1996, I led my first camp on the campus of Gadsden State Community College. I was twenty-two years old. I had served as a junior counselor in high school, a counselor throughout college, and even youth camp director one year. But designing the camp from top to bottom, and having it on our own terms, was big. Like every year, the youth came from across Alabama and all across the country. The group from Selma was a mishmash of young people from our local chapter and anyone Mrs. Sanders might have recruited in her travels. She was our biggest recruiter, which happily meant we were ever growing, but we had a small budget and an even smaller team, so it also meant sometimes we were spread a bit thin.

As an organization that recognized that young Black and Brown children were often criminalized and demonized, and rarely ever given the benefit of the doubt and space to grow, we prioritized accountability over punishment. The young people set the parameters for safety and decorum for the camps. They agreed on guidelines and created a council to address leaders who didn't follow them. It sometimes meant long nights of impromptu testimony and discussion about someone who had broken a guideline, but this system provided assurance that the leaders would be seen and heard and that consequences could come from a place of love, not harsh judgment. This approach was completely foreign to campers who were used to zero-tolerance policies and extreme punishment in other structured environments, and they would test the boundaries of our love and acceptance.

The young leader who pushed the boundaries the most during the summer of '96 was Heaven. She came to camp with the group of kids from Selma, but I didn't know her. She would have blended in with a sea of other prepubescent Brown faces if she hadn't come off the minibus fussing—loudly.

"I don't care who she is. She AIN'T *my* mama," was the first thing I heard as I approached the group of kids she had just arrived with. One of the adults escorting them was two seconds away from letting loose on Heaven. I saw the frustration in the escort's eyes and waved her away, turning my attention to the fussing girl.

"What's your name, sweetheart?" I asked her calmly.

"What? Why?" she asked, swerving her head around to get a closer look.

"Oh, I just need some help with something inside, will you come with me to help . . ." I trailed off, waiting for her to fill in her name.

"Heaven," she said, less loud now. Her voice lowered almost with anticipation that I would have something negative to say.

"Heaven," I repeated excitedly. "That's *beautiful*! Oh, I definitely need your help! Come with me."

I pulled two other young folks who I did know from the group, and they all followed me into the building.

"What we doin'?" one of the kids asked.

I had no idea, but they would never know that. I was thinking on my feet.

"Heaven, I need you to count the students who are coming into the building when this next bus comes in, okay?"

She had her face screwed up when I glanced at her.

"Count ALL'lem kids! Das a LOT! And these chir'ren don't know how to act."

She sounded like someone's old auntie, her voice a tad raspy. Her little accent tickled me. I turned and got a good look at her face. She may have sounded like a sixty-year-old woman who smoked a pack of Newports a day and had a hairstyle that made her look like she worked the last shift on the last register at the Winn-Dixie, but she had the sweetest little round, brown cherub face. Brow furrowed, she waited on me to give her further directions for this arduous task.

"You don't have to speak to anyone. Just stand here, and as the groups come in, start counting. You can ask them what county they are from and then write the county and the number down. I will bring you some paper and a pen." I was about to walk off when she interrupted me.

"What if they tell me to move on?" She had a seriousness that said she was ready to do her job well, which made me want to break into a smile, but I was trying to play it cool.

"Who?" I asked.

"I'ont know, one of dem," she said pointing out the door at the woman she had just been fussing with on the van.

"Listen, you stand right here and count and if anyone says anything to you—you tell them that Ms. Tarana put you here and you are doing a job for her." I sounded like a real camp director who could give that directive with authority.

"Das you, right? Is you in charge?" she wanted to verify.

"That's me, and yes, I am in charge," I smiled at her, feeling proud.

"Okay, den Ms.—whatchu said your name is?"

"Ms. Tarana, or Ms. Tee," I replied, a bit unsure of why I said that because I had not let any of the other kids shorten my name. But before I had time to think or correct myself, she had already decided.

"Oh, Imma call you Ms. Tee. That'll work!"

I chuckled a bit, said okay, and walked away thinking what a handful this one was going to be this summer. This was just day one.

Handful was an understatement. Heaven very quickly showed me, and everyone else at camp, that her behavior would continuously betray her name. By day two I had decided that she was going to be my special project. Every day, I would either be greeted by someone complaining to me about Heaven and her "attitude" or be ambushed by Heaven racing to tell on herself before someone else could. She was often loud, most of the time dripping with attitude and sarcasm, but rarely was she completely in the wrong. She reminded me so much of what I wanted to be at her age. She was angry, feisty, and didn't know why—almost like she was being compelled—but it was always in pursuit of some sort of justice. There was a righteous fury in her belly, and while I could easily sniff that out I couldn't yet figure out the why. If a counselor was talking to another camper in a way that she thought was outside of our accepted culture, she spoke on it. If a camper was treating another camper disrespectfully or in any way shady, she spoke on it. Heaven and I had more than a few heart-to-hearts and side conversations about her tone, attitude, and presentation. She *always* had something to say.

One night after lights-out, I came into the dormitory space right as Heaven was being reprimanded by one of our elders. The elders were revered figures in our lives. They had worked hard to mold and shape us. They wanted to pass on the vision they had laid out during the twenty-fifth anniversary of the Selma to Montgomery march and prepare us to lead the organization into the twenty-first century. When I saw Heaven and one of our more stern elders, Ms. Pitts, my heart jumped. I didn't want Heaven to say or do anything too egregious, and I didn't want a reprimand from Ms. Pitts to roll back any of the progress we had made so far. I jumped in as quickly as I could.

"Everything okay?" I asked, trying to erase any color in my voice.

"This young lady has told me that she is *not* going to bed because she is *not* sleepy!" Ms. Pitts was clearly annoyed.

"I don't want to go to bed. I want to read my thing," Heaven pleaded.

Ms. Pitts turned back to her. "That's very commendable, young lady, but now is not the time for reading; now is the time for sleeping!"

Heaven, who was always admiringly quick witted, shot back, "But y'all call it *steal away studying* so I want to steal away and read!"

I looked down and saw that Heaven was holding the Black history study guide all the young leaders received upon arrival. Each camper was put into a small group that would meet throughout the week to cover a section of the study guide. At the end of the week, there was an event based on what they had studied and the groups competed for prizes. We called them "steal-away study sessions." It was a reference to what enslaved people called "steal-away meetings." It was illegal for them to learn to read—an act that was punishable by death—so they snuck away under the cover of night to become literate. When I saw the book and heard her explanation to Ms. Pitts, it took everything I had not to burst into laughter.

"Okay, Heaven," I said, stifling my chuckle. "I need to talk to you anyway. Come with me."

"I'm in trouble?" she asked.

"No," I whispered, "just follow me so that you don't get in no trouble!"

We left Ms. Pitts shaking her head and walked back over to the main building. She sat in the office while I finished up some stuff and prepared to end the day and go to bed myself. We chatted about random things, and she asked me questions about stuff she didn't understand in the study guide.

"Heaven, are you liking camp?"

"Yes, ma'am. It's fun when these chir'ren ain't on my nerves," she said, rolling her eyes and erupting into laughter.

It had only been three or four days, but I adored this child. Her big, rosy cheeks and deep belly laughter made my whole heart light up. Maybe it was because she made me feel like I knew what I was doing. Or maybe it was because I knew what was happening. I was watching the transformation I had seen so many times before. The one that I went through standing in that big, open room in DC, and the one I knew so many of my 21C family had experienced at some point in their own journeys to being leaders. We called it the "21C spirit." It wasn't something anyone could fully explain, but we all agreed that we had it, basked in it, and were very protective of it. I was watching Heaven step into it with glee.

I'm sure it was what led me to say what I said next. "Well, you are one of us now, you are a 21st Century leader, and we are your family."

She stopped laughing and refocused on me. I had said that to other young people in one way or another. I felt like part of my role in the organization was as ambassador and success story. Not the "she finished high school and went on to college" kind of success—but the "she left a dark place and found community and purpose" kind of success. The 21st Century Youth Leadership Movement made me feel like I was good. Not just a good person, but good for something other than what I had been used for already. No one here knew that about me, and no one here cared. I wanted Heaven to experience that.

"We *family*?" Suddenly she looked more like the girl who got off the van a few days earlier. "We ain't family, Ms. Tee, now you ain't gotta say alladat!"

"Alla-what? We *are* family! We are here to take care of each other. You will meet people here that you will know for the rest of your life."

"But families is supposed to take care of you and feed you and . . . loooove you, no matter what!"

I stopped what I was doing, got real close to her face, and cupped her cheeks in my hands.

"You don't think I love you, Heaven," I said, locking eyes with hers. She looked like her little milk chocolate cheeks were going to melt into my hands. Before she could even answer, I continued, "but I do." And I kissed her on the forehead.

She just smiled. Beamed, really. She gave me a hug—a long side hug that made me start laughing again.

I gathered my things and we walked back to the dormitory so I could escort her to her room. I felt accomplished. I had started the week off thinking that this child named Heaven would be a hellion, and I was determined to love that out of her. Here we were just a few short days later and she was melting in my hands. This was the way I had been held by the elders in 21C. This was the way I had seen love shared and spread around when we gathered. And this was all I wanted Heaven to know. I didn't realize at the time how much more she needed to know.

The next day started just like every other day at camp. The young people gathered, exercised, ate, and had pep rally. After the pep rally we took a moment to explain what was on the schedule for that evening. Long-time campers knew what this announcement was about right away, and they were giddy and excited—especially the girls. New folks were baffled at all the excitement and started asking questions. That evening would be our annual "Sister to Sister" and "Brother to Brother" sessions. They were a long-held tradition at our camps that grew out of our natural inclination to gather and speak freely with the young people. This way, we set aside structured time, and the young leaders knew it was coming. When I was younger, Sister to Sister sessions were one of my favorite and most nerve-racking parts of camp. It was a space to bare all. The sessions were always filled with a lot of laughter and giggling. The elders and counselors opened the floor and allowed us to ask any questions we wanted.

Over the years, we had developed a rhythm. The night always started with silly "girly" questions about hair or clothes or music. Then one bold girl would ask a question about a boy, and the adults running the session would launch into the conversation. This was often where we learned who was doing what with which boys and who wanted to. We always had some confessions from the recently "deflowered" and the ones who were curious or maybe on the verge. And, without fail, there was eventually a story, a confession, a testimony, or some way that one of the girls revealed her experience with sexual or physical abuse. When I was a camper I was so close to that experience myself, and no part of me wanted to revisit it. But now I was a new person. A leader. And so when my sister leaders poured their hearts out, I listened, I cried, I comforted, I sometimes shrank away—but I never shared. My 21C family knew what I wanted them to know about me.

That night, we all gathered in the library for our session. The girls had all put on pajamas, and the room looked like a massive sleepover was about to take place. There were young girls sprawled all over, some in chairs, others lay out on blankets or cozied up in pairs. Every face glowed with anticipation. When I came into the space, a few of the girls got excited and started shouting out my name and clapping. I was the "cool" adult who gave it to them straight. I greeted them and scanned the room for Heaven. She was on the other side of the room, and we had a sea of girls between us, so I just waved and winked at her and then sat and joined the circle. I kept my eyes on her, though. I knew she had issues with a few of the girls at the camp because of her abrasive demeanor, and I wanted to be sure she was comfortable.

The night went like clockwork. There was a bunch of squealing and giggling and silly talk, and then we had a pretty robust conversation about menstrual cycles. I thought, "Oh, we might avoid a testimonial this year." But I spoke too soon. I don't know how it started, but in a matter of minutes, one of the girls was talking about being assaulted at school. She was asking the adults if an encounter she had with an older student was okay or not. The adults swung into action. We had all been here before, and each of us played a role. Mine was usually the check-in—asking if they needed to talk to someone and if they were okay to go home. We were committed to being better about taking responsibility for the young people in our care who were experiencing any kind of trauma. For all the good the organization did, sexual violence was its blind spot.

Years and years of girls spilling their innermost truths about their experiences, and 21C never employed a trained professional to oversee these sessions. Numbers of girls, and some boys, gave us clear indications that they may not have been safe at home, and we sent them back anyway, with no defense and no recourse. It remains in the front of my mind today. It is wildly irresponsible to make people feel comfortable enough to open up without being prepared with the resources to help them process their experiences and receive continued support. We were doing our best with the limited knowledge and resources we had at the time, but even then I wished we were doing more.

As it often did, that one confession led to others, and more girls shared their experiences openly. I became wrapped up in supporting them in the moment. I wrote names down, I passed out tissues to wipe tears, I checked in and comforted, almost on autopilot. At some point it occurred to me that I hadn't checked in with Heaven. My eyes darted around the room until I found her. She didn't see me looking at her because she was no longer there. She hadn't physically left, but even with all the upheaval and movement around her, she was perfectly still—emotionless. I looked at her face and posture, and I didn't have to see her eyes to know. *She was me.* I was transported right back to being fifteen or sixteen, sitting in a room full of crying teenage girls sharing horrible stories that I could never ever repeat, because I never allowed myself to confront the truths of what had happened to me. I would find a place to retreat in my mind, careful not to be so tuned out that folks felt the need to check on me. I would demure and become invisible. I was watching Heaven do it right before my eyes. She had faded into her own world of safety. The girl with a mouthful to say—ready to defend anyone she deemed defenseless—was doing her best to defend herself.

I didn't approach her. I just made sure to keep checking back throughout the rest of the night. We closed out the session, and the girls, most of them emotionally drained, went to bed.

The next morning I was back on my routine, and so was Heaven. Someone approached me and said that she had gotten into an argument at breakfast. When I got a report like this, I usually went and got her and either talked to her or gave her an assignment or somehow made sure the rest of her day went better. But that day I didn't. Later in the morning we passed each other going between the main building and the dorms, and as she walked by she loudly whispered, "I *need to talk to you.*" I felt my pulse quicken. I knew what she needed to talk about, and something in me—everything in me—couldn't have that conversation.

I mouthed back "Okay!" but in my mind I was already figuring out ways to get out of it. By the late afternoon it was obvious that I was avoiding her. The week was almost over, but there was no way I could keep this up for the rest of the time she was there. I didn't even fully understand why I was avoiding her, or at least I wouldn't let myself say it out loud in my head.

I was coming out of the cafeteria, not paying attention, and suddenly she was coming toward me.

"Ms. Teeeeee!" she screamed as she ran over and threw her arms around me.

I tried to feign a bit of excitement, but I had started to sweat.

"Where have you been?" She was exasperated. "I have to talk to you."

"I'm so busy today, girl. Can we talk later?" I asked, trying to pull her off me so I could walk away.

"No!" She was firm. "We need to talk *now.*"

My stomach was starting to turn.

She took my hand and pulled me to the side. As she held my hand, I realized that I was terrified.

She stood directly in front of me with eyes begging to confess. To confide. To release.

"Ms. Tee, last night . . . whew." She started, then stopped herself. "It was a LOT!"

I could feel my bladder pulsating against my pelvis.

"I just have to tell you about what happened to me . . . I never told nobody before."

I wanted to scream. Inside, I *was* screaming.

"It's like, my stepdaddy, really my mama's boyfriend," she continued. "He did stuff to me . . ."

I mostly only heard words and phrases after that: *nasty, don't like it, afraid, hate him, disgusting.*

I don't know how many minutes passed. I don't know how much of the story she had told. I just knew at some point I could not take another minute. This young girl, who reminded me so much of myself, was putting me right back where I didn't want to be—so I cut her off midsentence.

"Okay!" I must have said it more loudly than I thought because it clearly startled her. "Okay, Heaven, this is not my area. You need to talk to Ms. Malika."

"Ms. Malika?" Her face was awash with confusion. "Which one is that?"

Heaven's voice had softened, and I could tell she was trying to understand what was happening. She was trying to understand my reaction to her story.

"The one with the headwrap. I'll show you. She can help you better than me, okay?" I had already started physically moving away from her. I was good at moving away. Getting away. From this. All of this. I always got away.

But Heaven had not met me as an adult who ran away from her. She had met me as an adult who ran toward her. Who embraced her. Who told her she was family and that she loved her.

"Ms. Tee?" She sounded astonished. "You just gon' walk away like that?"

It felt like a knife had been plunged into my heart. The disappointment in her voice twisted the knife even deeper.

"No, baby, I'm not walking away. I am so busy right now and this is more for Ms. Malika to deal with." I knew the frustration was building in her chest, but I just wanted her to relent so that I could get away. I was going to lose my ability to breathe at any moment.

"Ms. Malika," she repeated staring at me, as if giving me a moment to reconsider.

"Yes, Heaven," I insisted, feeling the cowardice creep up the back of my neck.

She stared for a half beat more, still in disbelief, and simply said, "That's okay."

And then she turned on her heels and left—but not before shooting me one last glance. And although it was only a quick second, it was long enough for me to see that sweet little round, brown face with the big grin sour and curl the corner of her lips in disgust. The campers were starting to pour into the building for lunch now, but I never took my eyes off her back. As she disappeared into the crowd I saw her posture change. It was as if the armor we had worked to chip away was materializing again before my eyes.

I knew I was wrong.

I also knew I was terrified.

I was supposed to be the one changing lives.

I was supposed to be leading by example and showing them what was possible when you stepped into your potential.

And there I was, a fraudulent "after" picture.

I didn't want to do what I had done. I didn't expect a twelve-year-old to knock me off my square. I had been compartmentalizing and prioritizing my thoughts and emotions for many years at this point. Every move I had made, from becoming a 21st Century Leader to excelling in track and field to being a student activist to coming to work for 21C— every single positive step took me further from the negative parts of my life and recast me as a person who wouldn't have to deal with such things. Inside of five minutes, this child was threatening to undo the order I had created. While she was simply trying to lean into what I had promised her—family, connection, love—I was desperately trying to run away from all she reminded me of: betrayal, loss, shame. Inside, I was running from room to room like the house was on fire. And then my brain did what I had trained it to do. It went into protection mode.

You are not a social worker or a counselor, I insisted in the solitude of my mind.

As she was walking away from me, possibly forever, I kept thinking about her face when she finally got me to stop and listen. She knew what she was about to say to me, but there was no fear in her eyes. Instead, she looked relieved. I wondered where that courage came from. How had she managed to do the thing that I had still not figured out how to do with a head start almost double her twelve short years? I wondered how, at the very least, I had not been able to meet her at the apex of her courage.

In my early organizing training, our elders told us that to be an effective organizer you had to meet folks where they were. I had to find what was common between me and the folks I was trying to reach, and then let them know what skin I had in the game and how my work would help meet their most basic needs. It never occurred to me for a moment that those guidelines could be useful here. It didn't occur to me because I had never been here.

I was not thinking about what I had to give Heaven—just what I wanted to keep from her. After all, I didn't see my story as my gift, only as my shame. I knew what it felt like to know at least one other person understood what you'd been through. I could have been to her what Maya Angelou was to me, but instead I let her walk away. I let her leave me worse off than she met me.

It wasn't the details of what she experienced that most resonated with me. It was the feeling it left her with. The confusion, the questions, the anger, and the sadness. It was the need for a way out or a way forward. There was only one thing I was compelled to share the whole time she was talking, and it was like someone else was whispering it into my ears. Not me, Tarana, who was standing there desperately trying to be desensitized, but another version of me. One that was saying, *Tell her, she should know. Let her know what this feels like. Share yourself. Be who you said you are.*

And then it was just that one thing on a loop. *Tell her it happened to you too.*

Two days later, camp ended. It was now Heaven who was avoiding me, and I was so ashamed of what I had done that I let her. I asked Malika to seek her out and ask if she needed anything, but I didn't follow up with her myself. I was sorting through a range of feelings, but mostly I was wallowing in my cowardice. On the final day I decided I would be an adult and at least try to say goodbye and maybe apologize, but I couldn't find her. I asked around and found out that a small group of Selma kids had been picked up in a van and she was likely with them. She was gone, and suddenly it seemed like my life—and hers—depended on me righting this wrong. I asked some of the folks from Selma, and each sent me to another one, trying to figure out who she was connected to and how I could reconnect with her. I always came up empty. Days later, after camp ended, I was still thinking about her and feeling pangs of guilt and shame. I was trying to come to terms with what had happened between us, with what my response meant in relation to the work I said I wanted to do. That familiar feeling of being a fraud was creeping into my spirit, and I hated it. It made me think of the wisdom of our elder Uncle Ted, who cautioned us never to lie to the young leaders. He said sometimes you may have to hold back for their own sake, but don't ever lie. He explained that young people could sniff out deceit and inauthenticity like bloodhounds, and once they caught wind of it, there wasn't much you could do to turn it around. He said your credibility is your capital with young folks and you have to safeguard it. I wished so badly that I could have formed these rational thoughts that day with Heaven.

Now the question remained: What would I do next time? I began to obsess over how I would do the whole thing differently. I wrote down notes and played out conversations and practiced my delivery, but it felt flat to me. I went to the bathroom and tried to look in the mirror, but my brain could not sustain the scrutiny. I turned my head away several times before I made myself envision Heaven. I closed my eyes and conjured up her round, brown face. I stood in front of my sink, directly facing the mirror, with my eyes closed, then slowly opened them. It took a few tries, but eventually I was staring at myself. My armpits were tingling and my breathing was quick and heavy, but I made myself look at my reflection. I needed to find at least a piece of the courage Heaven had found. There was no one here but me, and I wanted to know that I could at least trust myself to stand in my truth. I slowed my breathing as best I could and felt the words inching their way from the pit of my stomach up toward the back of my throat, where they stopped. It felt like I might choke on them. I commanded myself to keep breathing. The words were almost there. I opened my mouth and they crept out, one small syllable at a time.

I *was raped.*
They *molested me.*
I *didn't want it.*
I *didn't like it.*
I'm *sorry.*

This is what I felt.

This is what I spent so much time ducking and dodging and twisting and contorting to avoid. These words. My truth.

It was a truth my mother never asked for.

It was a truth none of my family or friends ever knew.

It was a truth no one was there to validate.

It was a truth I ran from for so very long.

But it was a truth I knew I needed to unravel. If not for myself, for the love of the girls like me who could be saved. For the next girl like Heaven I would meet—and there would be so very many. It was out of my body for the first time and I was still alive. I was still standing—with my truth on the outside.

hypnotize

The moment I found out I was pregnant, I prayed I wasn't carrying a baby girl. I was so committed to the idea that I picked out dozens of names for the boy I hoped was in my belly. I was too nervous to find out the sex of my child, so I let the nurse tell my boyfriend, who was dying to know. I forbade him from telling me. I wanted my baby more than anything, but the thought of bringing a little girl into the world who might be subjected to my fate was horrifying. I wanted to save my future "her" from an unkind world filled with unkind men who saw a little girl like me as an ugly, nasty dishrag to be used and discarded.

I had spent many painful years feeling unprotected and shamed by my mother, not realizing that I was running up against the limits of her capacity to protect me—even her understanding of protection. As I got older, comparing notes with my girlfriends and listening to the stories of the little Black girls in my programs, I came to understand compounding shame. And it was almost always connected to an older Black woman in our lives. Many times, that woman was our mama or auntie or someone we held dear. For the most part, those women loved those girls like my mother loved me. They thought they were doing the right thing. I believe my mother did too.

Now I was pregnant and scared despite the euphoria I felt about becoming a mother. I thought if I had a little boy, he had a better chance at escaping my fate. He wouldn't be immune to unkindness, of course—I certainly had my anxieties about bringing a little Black boy into the world. But I was able to hold that fear. I was able to isolate those anxieties. I told myself that I could prepare my baby for the nastiness that awaited Black boys in America, even though I knew my heart couldn't handle the reality that too many of our boys are robbed of their innocence and walk through life with a target on their backs. But still, it felt different than the overwhelming fear of having a child who looked like me and dealt with the things I'd endured. The roaming hands of boys who didn't give a fuck that they didn't have permission to touch. The anger of men who didn't understand why I didn't want to give them my number or respond to their catcalls. Or the violent betrayal of those who would rather rob me of my innocence than take care of me. And so I didn't want to know the sex of this child. Ironically, I learned I was having a girl when my child's father let it slip during our breakup. As his words sunk in, my prayers to God changed. Now that I knew I was having a baby girl, I begged God that she at least didn't look like me.

The father of my child was my on-again, off-again high school boyfriend, Sean. He had relocated to Alabama from New York so we could be together while I was working with 21C. Our relationship had been tumultuous from the beginning. We were fifteen when we met. He had recently lost his mother to illness and I had lost mine to the man in her life. We were each other's escape from reality. He was a "bad boy" who had a tenuous relationship with rules and authority. He was miles away from the studiousness and discipline of my life between advanced classes, track, and other extracurricular activities, but he had a softer, sweet side. We had a young, wild love that kept us on our toes—and on our backs. He was an intellectually curious free spirit longing for structure, but the adults around didn't give it to him. I was grateful that someone took a real interest in me, and he was grateful to have a breather from the street persona he was caught up in. We lived in our own world—in our little bubble, as we called it—as an escape from our realities, but at some point I became blinded to the toxicity that had slowly set up residence in his heart.

We were just kids when I got pregnant—I was twenty-three and he was three months from it. Neither of us had good examples of what a loving, caring, safe relationship between two adults looked like. My mom was a fighter. I had witnessed her in full-blown tussles with men, sparring as if they were mortal enemies, and then they'd share laughs and smiles and sweet kisses like nothing had happened. His life wasn't much different.

When we first moved in together, we had our share of drama, but what couple didn't? Even though we dated somewhat consistently through high school and college, when he showed up in Alabama, I was no longer the young girl he knew. We had been long distance and he hadn't fully met the new me who was emerging as I found my way on my own, away from the judgment and shame of my life back in New York. The toxicity of our relationship had been there all along, but the teenage version of me who was in love with this boy chose to overlook it. Once, when we were in high school, he'd lured me up to the roof of his apartment building to tell me that he would throw me off and then jump if I moved away for school. He grabbed me and held me over the ledge, professing his love while I begged and pleaded with him. When he stopped, I comforted *him* as he cried over what had just transpired. I didn't see this as violence because I thought I knew violence. I explained it away as an extreme expression of his love for me, not making space to consider it manipulation.

I was stronger now, and I wasn't going to stand for that kind of "love" anymore. I would lean into what I learned from my mother and my aunt and all the other women around me growing up, and so I decided I would fight back the next time he tried some shit like that. I was determined to show him that my mother didn't raise no punk—which is exactly what I said to him as we both lay breathless on the cold, hard tile of the kitchen floor after a knockdown, drag-out fistfight in our Alabama apartment. Nothing in particular had started the fight, but it ended with him smacking at me one too many times and my fist connecting with his jaw and the back of his head and wherever else I could manage until we both passed out from sheer exhaustion.

"You fucking crazy, Tee. You fucking fighting like a wild animal and shit," he said, trying to catch his breath.

"I'm not crazy," I responded. I was barely able to catch my own breath. "You just mad because my mother ain't raise no punks!"

We didn't always have a volatile relationship. We fell in love because we filled a void for each other. I was a version of myself that I didn't get to explore often: soft, silly, and sexy. Sean had the space to stretch himself beyond the limits of his circumstances. He was open and unguarded with me. Not many Black boys had space to be that. It also helped that we enjoyed the same things: Knicks basketball, hip-hop, gangster pictures, and dreaming big. It made us feel connected, deeply connected, and we were incredibly protective of our bubble.

That was then.

The day before I found out that I was pregnant, I had gone to the city council meeting to watch as the racist mayor and council president of Selma conspired to take the power to appoint city officials from the incoming council. It was the first time in the city's history that we would have a majority Black city council. For months we had been protesting this travesty, which would give the mayor and council president the ability to appoint people to significant roles like chief of police and comptroller. But today—the day the council was to vote on the appointment powers—one of the Black council members was absent. The vote would have to be a draw. We expected all the other Black members to vote in the affirmative, so it was on the record that they wanted their powers back, but to our surprise two of the four councilmembers abstained from voting.

I jumped out of my seat and cursed out the turncoat council members. We had done so much organizing, only to come to this. The mayor ordered the chief of police to arrest me, and he and two deputies dragged me out of the council chambers. I went to the city jail—a pretty commonplace occurrence among us organizers—and waited for my bail to be posted.

It was posted within the hour and I hustled over to the law office—not to meet my attorney but to attend a strategy session about our next move. From there, I went to the National Voting Rights Museum to help the other volunteers get ready for the Footprints to Freedom ceremony that night. The copier at the museum broke right in the middle of me printing programs, so I had to run back over to the law office to finish them. I had promised Sean that we would cook dinner together, so we met up to go get groceries—I was a little annoyed he didn't volunteer to do this on his own—and drop them off at home before going back to the museum for the program. When the event was done, I was very tired. This was my life in Selma—I was always ripping and running around town. That was the work. I was used to it.

The second I opened the door to the house a wave of nausea hit me. I figured it was just my body telling me to sit my ass down for once. I let Sean do most of the cooking as I sat and buttered the rolls, mindlessly watching the TV. When he came to get the rolls, he looked in the bowl and there was just one left. He grabbed the bowl, staring down at the lone roll. I had been unconsciously buttering and eating them.

He raised his eyes to meet mine. "You're pregnant."

First thing the next morning, I went out and bought a test. I dreaded taking it. I had been pregnant once before about two years earlier and I'd miscarried.

When I walked in the apartment with the test, Sean was gesturing wildly for me to get to the TV. Two weeks prior, Biggie Smalls, our favorite rapper, had been murdered, and the music video for his new single was about to drop on MTV. I figured I had a few seconds to sneak off to the bathroom and take the test—I was that convinced it was negative. I plopped down on the toilet and peeled open the foil packaging. I read over the instructions: One line meant not pregnant; two lines meant pregnant. Pee on the stick. Wait three minutes. *Cool.* I did just what the directions said. When the test immediately revealed two lines, I threw the plastic stick in the sink and closed my eyes.

"Okay, God," I said, still sitting on the toilet. "I'm just going to wait because I know this is negative, and I just need to follow the directions and wait the full three minutes."

I sat with my eyes closed until Sean started screaming for me to come out of the bathroom. I pulled myself together, grabbed the test, and ran to the living room. I was just in time for the video opening. Biggie and Puff were on a speedboat jetting across the water. Biggie was smiling in a way we had never seen before—they both looked so fly. We were on the edge of the couch, and when it was over MTV ran it back again. We watched, singing along to each other. When it was done, my boyfriend sat back on the couch and asked what had happened with the test.

I uncurled my fist from around the stick and looked down. "Oh, two lines."

I looked up at him and threw up two fingers.

He jumped up and grabbed the test and started shouting, jumping on the couch. *"My baby is having my baby!!"* he screamed, then ran right out the door to our big, screened-in porch, yelling out into the stillness of midday, *"MY BABY IS HAVING MY BABY!!!!!"*

I called him back into the house. He came in and grabbed my hands and started singing the little ditty he had just made up. *"My baby's having my baaaa-by, my baby's having my baaaa-by!"* I had never seen him so happy.

My insides were turning upside down with nerves, but his enthusiasm was so infectious that I eventually joined him in song—adding a tweak to the lyric: *"I'm having my baby's baaaa-by! I'm having my baby's baaaa-by!"* We wore ourselves out singing and dancing, and eventually fell asleep fully entwined in one another.

The joy was short lived.

Within a week of finding out about the baby, he changed. We were back to arguing all the time and he was staying out more, getting strange numbers on his beeper. Two months into my pregnancy, I was growing weary. I tried to focus on work, but it was difficult with all the drama at home. The tension was as thick as day old grits in our house, and by the end of my first trimester, things came to a head. We were communicating in grunts and half sentences most of the time, and his presence was starting to make me sick. One afternoon, as I was rushing around trying to get ready for my girlfriend's baby shower, he started "smelling his piss," as old Black folks like to say, and decided to confront me.

He started off reasonably enough. "We need to talk, Tee."

"I can't talk now; I am doing Malika's baby shower." I was short and direct, and that set him off.

"It's always something or somebody else! It's never me! What about me? I need you!" He was screaming at the top of his lungs, which honestly I was used to. We often communicated at that decibel. But I wasn't going to stand and listen to his bullshit. I brushed past him and headed to the kitchen. He caught up and grabbed me by my wrists, pushing me back up against the wall. His speed and aggression caught me off guard.

"What the fuck are you doing?" I screamed. "Get the FUCK offa me!"

"No, you gon' talk to me," he snarled through gritted teeth, pressing harder into me as I tried to wrangle out of his grip. When I broke loose, I jerked my arm back as if I were going to punch him. We had been in this place so many times. I knew that he knew I would defend myself. I waited for him to cover his face, or move away from me, but he didn't budge. Instead, he lunged for my wrists again, and that's when it hit me. I was pregnant. I was pregnant and vulnerable—and he knew it. I had seen my mom and step-dad fight enough times to know that fighting and domestic violence were two different things. Domestic violence was what happened to Farrah Fawcett in *The Burning Bed.* Up until that moment, I thought it was what happened to women who couldn't defend themselves. I thought it happened to victims. I was a fighter, and what my boyfriend and I did was fight. Until the moment came where I couldn't. Standing there, my first instinctual need to protect my child rocked me to my core. I relented.

The moment my maternal instincts kicked in, his instinct to attack did too. The second I stopped struggling, he dragged me into the living room and threw me on the couch. First, he sat next to me, leaning on my chest so I couldn't move. I did my best never to think about the attacks on my body, but now the memories flooded back. I didn't want to fight him anymore, but I could not stand the feeling of being pinned down with no escape, so I tried to wiggle out from under him. That just made him madder. He snatched me by my long box braids and wrapped the pony-tail around his fist as if he were coiling a garden hose. When he reached the top of my head, he pulled me from the couch to the floor and positioned me so I was hemmed between his legs, my head resting on his knees and his legs draped over my shoulders. We sat like that for over two hours while he blabbed on and on about how much he loved me, and how this new family of ours had to come first, and how he would kill me and our unborn child if I left. He talked about how I made him feel alone and inadequate after he left Maryland and relocated to Selma for me. He screamed and cried, and he threatened, and he pleaded, and he professed. He carried on as my head pounded with pain from how tightly he held my braids. I sat perfectly still. I spoke soft and sweet to him, feeding his ego with the platitudes he desperately wanted to hear. I promised he was the only man I had ever loved and could ever love. I told him I was in full agreement that our family had to come first now. I said all the things that soothed him when he acted this way, like that time on the roof of his building. I fed him memory after memory of us in happier times. I reminded him of the sex we would have after our episodes and the happiness we found despite how broken we were, together and apart.

My whispers of sweet nothings and promises made him loosen his grip. I kept still as I counted the steps between me and the front door. I had never gotten fully dressed for the baby shower. I had on a bra and a button-up shirt and slippers and nothing but my panties on underneath. I couldn't go far, but my girlfriend lived maybe five or six blocks away. I could do that in slippers, I thought.

He let up just a bit more, and I felt some of my braids fall from around his fist. He went to adjust his body on the couch, and I jumped up and ran—but the door was locked, and it felt like I didn't have enough time to fumble with getting it open. I looked down, suddenly aware of how naked I was, and turned and ran into the bedroom. I threw myself on the bed and began crying uncontrollably. It was the most scared and lost I had felt in a long time. He walked in and knelt down on the bed next to me. He had completely changed in a matter of seconds. He immediately began apologizing—he was talking so much that I don't even remember what words he said, but he was pleading with me to forgive him. I had been in this honey trap here before. He would do something foul and fucked up, and when I reacted with tears or anger he would apologize profusely and demand that I accept his apology in the moment. I wouldn't have any time to process what had happened. I wasn't sure how to respond to this outpouring of remorse. Even in our worst fights or craziest moments I had never seen him like he was that day. I knew that, with this baby in my stomach, I never wanted to see it again.

I could hear him in between my screams, speaking in the most gentle, comforting tone.

Baby, please stop crying—you're going to hurt the baby.

Tee, you gotta calm down or you will make yourself sick.

How could he switch gears like this? Would he switch back if I didn't stop crying? I was too tired to play his games. Between the searing headache from the tension on my scalp and the exhaustion from crying and his empty words, I fell asleep. I awoke feeling disoriented. I couldn't remember falling asleep. I only remembered crying. My stomach was doing flips and I had to pee, but I could barely muster the strength to get out of bed. He was still lying next to me. He felt me stir and it brought him back to attention. He got up on all fours and hovered above me and started gently caressing my face. My body went rigid at his touch. I don't know if I was frightened or disgusted, but I knew I didn't want his hands on me.

I needed to get away, but it felt impossible. I managed to shift my body a bit, but I was lying on a pile of clothes, so I couldn't scoot up from under him easily. He started kissing me and tried to put his tongue in my mouth. I lay still. He started kissing me on my breast through my partially unbuttoned shirt. I remained still. It took him no time to get to my panties. I twisted my body and tried holding my legs closed, but he opened them and started licking me.

"Stop," I said, thankful to my vocal cords for finally pushing out the word.

I knew he heard me because he laughed. "You don't want me to stop."

But I did. Nothing about this was pleasurable.

"Stop!" I said it louder this time.

"Aight, I'll stop," he said. And he stood up from the bed.

My skin crawled as I tried to muster the strength to get up and go to the bathroom. I needed water on my face and in my system. But then my brain focused, and I realized what was happening. He had stood up to take off his pants. And his underwear. I knew what was coming next. I have gone over this moment again and again in my head. I take each piece and dissect it. In my mind, I step into the bedroom like a crime scene investigator, scanning the room for information, but mostly staring intensely from my face to his face, then at both of us.

What. Should. I. Do?

What should I do?

What should I have done?

What I did was nothing.

Nothing.

I couldn't even slide off the bed before he climbed back on top of me and used his knee to separate my legs. He put his penis inside of me like he had done a million times before.

And he . . . had sex with me. At least, that is how I told the story in my head for the sake of my child and my sanity. I had to tell it that way.

I cried the whole time. I lay still the whole time. He had to know I didn't want it.

But maybe I did want it?

Sometimes my mind convinces me that I did because I didn't *stop* it. Sometimes I believe that he didn't know. But how could I have stopped him, gotten out of the apartment safely, and still had a father for my child? Even then I knew that *this* moment couldn't live out in the world. So when he was done I turned over and forced myself to fall back asleep.

The events of the previous night must have made him think that things were smoothed over. He was prancing around the house, making breakfast and asking me random questions. But I knew what I had to do. I got up, showered, got dressed, and left the house without saying a word to him. That went on for a few days. I stayed out of the house as much as possible, and we barely spoke when I was there. Sometimes I walked to my office downtown, sometimes I walked to one of my girlfriend's houses, and sometimes I just walked around aimlessly, always with my headphones and Discman. Always listening to Mary J. Blige's *My Life* album. I kept "Be Happy" on repeat. The lyrics were so simple, but they felt like prayer to me in that moment. *"All I really want is to be happy, to find a love that's mine, it would be so sweet."* That was all I wanted for my life and for the life of this baby growing inside me, and I knew it was missing. Why wasn't I happy? More importantly, what was this unhappiness going to do to my baby?

About a week after the incident, I came home midday to find him there, as usual, but this time I needed to talk to him. I took a deep breath and told him I wanted him to leave my house.

"Leave?" He had the audacity to be incredulous and it pissed me off. "With a baby on the way—*now* you want me to leave? Okay, Tee, because that makes sense!"

I stood there quietly staring at him. I knew if I said too much I would end up talking myself out of my decision or letting him manipulate me into shrinking.

"So, when is this supposed to happen? Now? I'm supposed to pick up and leave now? And where am I going?" His tone was condescending as fuck, but I knew him well enough to know that he was actually shook. What made him the angriest was that he knew me well enough to know I was dead-ass serious. I wanted him out.

"How long do you need?" I asked him.

"I don't know—a week, two weeks . . . This shit is crazy, Tee. We havin' a baby!"

"You were not thinking about our baby when you were pushing and shoving me last week, were you," I reminded him.

"Nah, Tee, don't do that. You know that was my temper. You forgave me for that," he said, falling into his slick double-talk. "You can't do that."

I was struck by the word *forgave*. Did he think what transpired between us was me forgiving him? My stomach churned. I was disgusted by him.

"I just need you to go. A week is fine."

I needed to end the conversation. I could feel the confines of my fear tugging at me. I didn't want to waiver or cry or let him see me falter in any way because he would have pounced and spun the web of sweet charm that I had found irresistible for so long.

"Fine, Tee. I'll go." He turned away from me and left the room.

I grabbed my purse and ran back out of the door.

I got about a block away before I sat down on the front steps of a house for sale. I needed to catch my breath. I reached in my purse and pulled out a book I had been carrying around with me for weeks. I had just discovered an author by the name of Iyanla Vanzant. She was a Black woman who talked about Black women having value and needing peace. Her work was a comfort to me because it married the wisdom of the elder women in my life and the wisdom of the Gospel that guided my life. I had read *The Value in the Valley* and then picked up its companion book called *Faith in the Valley*. It was a small book with lessons and affirmations that bolstered the takeaways from its sister book. I would read a few pages every day—on the way to work, at lunchtime, before bed, and sometimes in moments when I was looking for guidance or clarity, like now.

I flipped to a random page, landing on 211. At the top left of each page there was a statement and on the top right, two words, with a longer passage at the bottom. On this page it said, "I know you think I'm crazy," on the left and had the words "Illumination" and "Inspiration" on the right. The passage read

*Finding the way to joy, peace, abundance, health
and balance requires an examination and evaluation
of everything you cherish. In the midst of your
evaluation, the Holy Spirit will step in and separate
that which is false from that which is true; that which
is necessary from that which no longer serves any
purpose in your life.*

*Separation from that which is familiar and cherished
is frightening. Yet the Holy Spirit is a spirit of light
which will reveal the darkness of things you have
held on to. When the darkness is revealed, what you
once cherished will look different! In some cases, it
will act different! The truth is nothing is different.
In the process of evaluation, the presence of the Holy
Spirit gives you the ability to see things in a new light.
Hopefully that light will set you free.*

At the very bottom of the page, it simply read,
"Everything looks different in the light of the spirit." And it
did. Everything looked different after the previous week. I
had been trying to twist this man's debilitating mix of toxicity, unresolved trauma, and longing for belonging into love
since before I could even understand what I was up against.
I genuinely felt connected to him, but in that moment, with
another human being growing inside of me, I felt more connected to my child. I was more invested in my child having
a life free of the things that I was just starting to myself
untangle from. When it came down to it, I chose not to close

my eyes to what was clear. I chose to see what was different. And I chose my baby.

The day he left was still hard. I thought I was going to crumble into a million particles of dust. The last thing he said before he left was, "Tell my daughter that I love her." That's how I found out the sex of the baby. Him breaking his promise before driving out of my life.

another storm

With the father of my child gone, I decided to head back to New York right after my baby, Kaia, was born. I had been missing my family while I was living in Selma, but that feeling faded after a brief stint in my mother's house. My mother and I had long made peace, but I needed to make different moves to give my child the life that I had been plotting and planning even before the moment we met. Plus, New York was so expensive and the work I wanted to do paid so little. I couldn't see a path forward that would allow for me to provide my child with the kind of life I wanted for us both. I was back in Alabama before Kaia's second birthday.

In Selma, Kaia and I eventually settled into a loft apartment above the building of the organization I ran, the Black Belt Arts & Cultural Center (BBACC), which had reopened in a new location post–Hurricane Katrina in 2005. We were now in downtown Selma in a storefront the Sanders family owned. The building had formerly been a karate school, so it was set up to house students, and the loft used to be occupied by the former owner of the school. The space reminded me of some of the posh apartments in upscale parts of New York like Tribeca or SoHo, minus the posh. It was a huge, twelve-hundred-square-foot raw space that the previous owner had done his best to make more homelike. The short, dark, narrow flight of steps leading up to the apartment were so daunting that it seemed like they were surely leading to a den of iniquity. But the first thing you'd see upon entering were gorgeous, deep-set windows that started right where the far wall met the ceiling and ended just above the hardwood floors with enough space to sit comfortably. There was a kitchenette in the back with a U-shaped countertop that held the sink, dishwasher, and stove. Toward the back of the house was a makeshift room with walls that didn't quite reach the ceiling, but a door created the illusion of privacy. Right behind the makeshift room in the far-left corner was a bathroom, and in the far-right corner was another door that led to an old lift leftover from when the space had been a warehouse around the turn of the century. The lift surprisingly still worked, since it was powered by a pulley system, but I was careful to keep that door secured so my curious child would not venture into potential danger. The space was sorely in need of a renovation, with several old, rotted floorboards and ancient systems for heating and cooling that made the temperature fluctuate wildly.

The year before the storm had been a rough one. While there had been no shortage of work to do in our community, there was very little money to do it. At the time, I was working three jobs to make ends meet. In 2004, finally pursuing my passion for writing, I applied for and was accepted into a journalism fellowship program at Vanderbilt University. The program, Freedom Forum Diversity Institute, trained midcareer professionals of color to be journalists and then placed them in newsrooms across the country. It required I spend three months in Nashville, but it was worth it. I came back to Selma and landed a job at the *Selma Times-Journal*, working with John Gullion, who would become my journalism mentor. As excited as I was to finally be a professional writer, I was not prepared for the realities of a small-town newsroom, including the pay, which hovered just above minimum wage. I worked full time at the Journal but split my day in half. From 8:00 a.m. to 2:00 p.m., I was in the newsroom or in the field, working as a reporter and copy editor. At 2:00, I would leave and make my rounds to various schools across the city, picking up students, including my own child, for BBACC's after-school program, in which I became the "African Dance Lady" to about twenty to thirty kids. Although our arts and culture program was more than a dance program, we were most popular for our African dance instruction. One of my most enduring memories of that time is of children screaming, "*HERE COME THE AFRICAN DANCE LADY!!!*" as I pulled up in front of their schools in BBACC's rickety white van. What followed was a swarm of kids running full speed toward the van from whatever spots they had huddled in to await my arrival. After the program was over, I dropped all the children off at their homes, and then would head to the National Voting Rights Museum, my third job, to finish up the day. That way, my child could lie in one of the exhibit rooms while I finished my journalism work or chipped away at some project for the museum.

I wasn't on a regular salary at the museum during this time; it was more of a eat-what-you-kill situation where I raised the money I needed to do the projects that they needed. I did receive a small stipend every two weeks for running the Black Belt Arts & Cultural Center, even though the organization had limited funding. As broke as I was during this time, I was content with my life and my work. Actually, money really wasn't my biggest problem. I always had enough for food and I had enough community in Selma that it would have been statistically impossible for me or my child to starve. Community was what undergirded Selma; it was the glue. One of the most important members of that community was the museum director, Joanne Bland, or Ms. Ann, as we affectionately called her. She was like a surrogate mother to me but also an icon in her own right. Ms. Ann and her sister, Lynda Lowery, who was the youngest marcher beaten on the Edmund Pettus Bridge on Bloody Sunday, had made a name for themselves as keepers of the movement history. Ms. Ann, who was there holding her sister's bludgeoned head in '65, gave a legendary historical tour of Selma that brought guests to the museum from across the world. She was always just Ms. Ann to us, though. She taught me so much about adult life, from how to cook to how to set boundaries. Ms. Ann, along with the rest of the staff, was like family. It felt good to flit across Selma from the museum to the Sanders's law offices, which were only a seven-minute walk away, and then back to the Black Belt Arts & Cultural Center. My child and I were always greeted with love and affection. I knew I could safely leave Kaia at any one of these locations while running errands or tending to some business. My community had earned that thing that I gave out so sparingly: trust.

But something shifted over the next year.

Kaia and I were at Jubilee, the annual three-day festival celebrating and commemorating the events that took place in Selma during the voting rights movement. It was formally called the Bridge Crossing Jubilee, but locals just called it Jubilee. I'd spent the last six months helping to coordinate it. Kaia was just seven at the time, but I loved having them there. We were surrounded by people who had known my kid since birth and me most of my life. I felt completely comfortable around them, and there was plenty of help when my focus was elsewhere.

I was charged with overseeing the festival's concert. That year's act was Southern hip-hop act 8Ball and MJG, and they were two hours late. While we waited for them to arrive, several of my friends milled about backstage, including Mrs. Sanders's son, Kindaka, or "Doc," who was like a brother to me, and several of his boys who I was also close to. One guy,

Malik, who was an extension of the crew, was a childhood friend of Doc's. Apparently he had been dealing with some mental health challenges, but his friends embraced him in spite of whatever was going on, and that day he was allowed to come backstage. Shortly after showing up, he became a menace. A fight nearly broke out because he said something inappropriate to one of my friend's wives and a couple of other women. I asked that he be escorted out, but in the blur of dealing with my growing issue with the headliners, I didn't follow up to ensure that he wasn't let back in. By the time the group finally arrived, the crowd was about to boil over. The group's manager, sensing they had the upper hand, started making demands before they would take the stage. I had Kaia and my niece, Princess, with me backstage. I turned to the kids and told them to stay right where they were. Both children obediently agreed, and I went to deal with this crumbling show. Ten minutes later I felt a tug at my shirt, and I turned to see my baby, Kaia, staring up at me with big, round, teary eyes and a small brown face that looked like the blood was drained from it.

"Baby! What's the matter?" I asked, my heart racing.

Kaia could not speak. I had no way of knowing what was happening and I had never seen them this way.

My niece had come up behind Kaia and spoke. "That man was bothering her, Auntie," Princess said, pointing. My eyes followed her little arm and landed on Malik, who was standing in the crowd. The rage raced up from my chest and burst into my head so fast it had nowhere to go but out.

"Who? *HIM?*" I screamed, pointing directly at Malik. My booming voice made him look in my direction and he started walking toward us. When Kaia saw him coming, my frightened baby leaped behind me. Just as Malik got within my reach, I pulled Kaia from behind me and confirmed, *"Is THIS the man that was bothering you?"* By this time, folks had begun to pay attention and my brother Doc was making his way to see what was up. Kaia, who was still quietly crying, nodded yes. It seemed like Malik wanted to say something— maybe to defend himself or apologize but most likely to deny—but none of it mattered because as soon as my baby nodded yes, I turned and punched Malik dead in his fucking face. I didn't know what he had done, but it didn't matter. I knew my child and I had never seen that depth of horror in their normally bright, dancing eyes. Before I could swing again, Doc grabbed me and another guy grabbed Malik. I fell apart, screaming like Sofia in *The Color Purple* for someone to get the girls to safety. Several police officers were back- stage serving as crowd control, and they came running over. Someone must have told them that I had assaulted Malik— who was the son of the local municipal judge—and they started pulling on me as if they were going to arrest me. I was yelling at the top of my lungs that he touched my daugh- ter, and they quickly let me go and started to detain him. Doc had Princess and Kaia taken away from the scene. In the end, since no one knew exactly what had happened, the police didn't arrest Malik and instead sent him on his way.

I had an awards ceremony to attend right after the con- cert, so I tried to collect myself and left the backstage area. I was supposed to present a Freedom Flame award to the leg- endary Chuck D of Public Enemy, and my uncle Neal, who was a huge Public Enemy fan, had come down from Atlanta to attend. I didn't have time to shower and change into the nice, ceremony-appropriate outfit I had laid out—I barely had time to even process what had just occurred before it was time to get onstage. I took the stage, lying to the audience, telling them that I had decided to keep it hip-hop by wearing a fitted Yankee hat, jeans, T-shirt, and Timbs instead of something fancy. I stumbled my way through a speech thanking Chuck for giving my generation a movement soundtrack similar to that of the sixties, and then I hurried offstage and waited for the soonest moment I could slip out without being noticed. My uncle's exit was my chance.

I saw him make his way to the back of the room toward the door, and I got up to follow him. I slipped through the door, and he turned around, excited that he got a chance to see me before he got on the road to Atlanta, but his face quickly fell as he registered my angst. Being ever tuned in to what was happening with me, he immediately sensed something was wrong and began asking if I was alright. My head started to spin and I could feel my face burning up. I felt like I was seven and standing in front of my stepdad, Mr. Wes, again. I knew that if I detailed the events from earlier in the evening that my uncle would not rest until he put hands on Malik. He was my protector in a lot of ways and that protection naturally extended to Kaia at birth. He was also a changed man—a teacher, a father, and a husband— but he had been in the streets at one point in his life, and the streets are never too far out of reach.

I hesitated, unsure of whether to confess the day's events, but ultimately, I knew I wouldn't. The piece of shit who had assaulted my child was not worthy of potentially upending my uncle's life just to snuff his out, so I lied, again. I brushed off his concern, saying I was fine, just a little tired. This time, though, I wasn't a seven-year-old making an adult decision; I was an adult doing what I knew was right in the moment.

It wasn't until later that night, when things had calmed down, that Kaia told me what happened backstage. Malik had come up and stood next to where the kids were standing, on the side closest to Kaia. When Kaia asked Princess to scoot down because Malik was standing too close, he also scooted down, staying a breath away from Kaia. He then bent down and whispered that he could "*show her something that she had never seen before*" and began to rub up and down on Kaia's thigh. It was at that point that full-on panic kicked in and both Kaia and Princess ran over to get me. The story made me want to curl up in a ball. I was filled with both the urge to cry and plot a torturous death for him, but I did neither. Instead, I assured my child that he would never bother them again and that they were safe from harm, because that is what I believed.

It wasn't long before everyone in our circle knew what had happened with Malik and Kaia at Jubilee. If they hadn't been there in person to witness some part of it, they had heard some version of the story. And that is why I was so surprised a month later to pull up to the museum and find Malik chilling outside. Unfortunately, Kaia saw him first. I was paying attention to parking the car when Kaia let out a scream and slid out of the seatbelt, cowering on the car floor. I was so startled that I didn't think to look outside. I just kept asking my baby, "What's wrong? Baby, what's the matter? What spooked you?" And then I saw him. He was leaning on the ledge of the Gathering Place, an extension of the museum located right next door, smoking a cigarette. My entire body flushed. I couldn't decide which impulse was the strongest—to scream, run up on his ass, or peel out of the parking lot and get my child out of there as fast as possible. I was still trying to make sense of my thoughts when Ms. Ann came outside. I rolled down the window to call her over to the car.

"Ms. Ann! What is *he* doing here?" I whispered loudly.

Ms. Ann, who nobody would describe as the whispering kind with her deep, gravelly voice, loudly replied while looking directly at Malik, "I don't know. He said he was sent over here from the law office to do some work, but I told him to get the hell outta here and don't come back. I *guess* I must have stuttered cuz he still out here looking as stupid as ever!" Malik began walking down the street. I pulled Kaia into the front seat and realized my baby had urinated through their clothes. I was devastated. How scary it must have been to see a person who harmed you in a place that represented safety. I took Kaia home to change and then drove back to the museum. I needed to know what had happened.

I barged through the doors. "Ms. Ann, what was he doing here?!"

"I don't know," she assured me. "He came prancing his lil ass in here talking 'bout they told him to come roun' here from the law office for some work, like that mean something to me!"

"But who would send him over here after what he did to Kaia? That doesn't make sense." I was baffled. It was commonplace for either Hank or Rose to try and accommodate folks from the community who needed to make some extra cash. Local guys knew that the Sanders always had something to clean, lift, unload, or distribute. Most of the guys who came around looking for odd jobs were from a small crew of usual suspects, but I had never seen Malik in that number.

"Who sent him?" I demanded, but I already knew the answer.

"Rose," Ms. Ann answered. "Rose told him to come over here."

Even though I knew it was her, my heart still plummeted as I stared at Ms. Ann disbelievingly. Mrs. Sanders had been friends with Malik's mom before her untimely death when he was just a kid. I knew she felt a sense of responsibility to look out for her friend's children. But in that moment, what I didn't know was why she didn't feel that same sense of responsibility for me.

From the time I met Mrs. Sanders when I was fifteen years old at that first camp in DC, I had been enamored with her. She was one of the most formidable women I had ever encountered. I had never experienced a person who could hold both righteous rage and uproarious delight. She was the definition of a supernova. Widely thought of as a legal genius, she could also compose music, sing, and play the piano. She was always sharp and rarely did anything slip past her—and if it did she made sure to double back and get it.

I didn't just look up to her and value her wisdom; I wanted to be her, and if I couldn't, I definitely wanted to please her. It was important to me that Mrs. Sanders see me as loyal and committed. Her validation was one of the driving forces for my tireless commitment to community. In Mrs. Sanders's eyes, you were only as valuable as what you sacrificed for the cause—her cause, that is, whatever it was at the moment. From the days of high school when I faithfully completed her monthly Goldstar leadership assignments, to volunteering at the museum and canvassing for Senator Sanders's campaigns in college, to now running the after-school program for the Black Belt Arts & Cultural Center for less than a living wage, I wanted Mrs. Sanders to see me as valuable so that maybe I would see myself that way too.

But that was my issue, and I knew it. And because I knew it, I was determined to make sure that my child—who I saw as valuable and raised to feel valued—was not exposed to anyone who saw or treated them differently. I was livid. This wasn't the first time that I felt like she had chosen to side with a boy or man accused of sexual misconduct. At 21C leadership camp, there had been a professor who taught us about Black history, and he had been rumored to have raped a girl at camp. He returned several times over the years, even after the rumors, until many of us started to believe it must not have been true. Then, there was a member of Mrs. Sanders's own family who had been repeatedly accused of sexual violence and somehow had never faced consequences—either legally or within our community.

I was not about to let this bell go unrung, though. I went straight to Mrs. Sanders's office to confront her. I showed up with all my anger, but she professed innocence. She told me that she didn't know exactly what had happened and had only heard that Malik and I "got into it" at the Jubilee.

"Why would you send him to the museum, my place of employment, if you knew we 'got into it'?" I was breathing heavily as she sat calmly behind her desk.

"I can't stop that boy from eating just because *you're* mad at him, Tawana. Who knows why you get mad and go off on folks," she said. "And why would I want to harm Kaia?"

It was classic Faya Rose Touré Sanders gaslighting.

I was stunned and offended. For Mrs. Sanders, diffusing and shutting down an argument was an artform and she was a savant. I left her office feeling silenced, and deeply unsettled. The feeling crept up on me like a small drumbeat, a tapping hidden somewhere in my spirit. I couldn't pinpoint it exactly, but I recognized it. I had definitely felt this feeling while growing up, but I had ignored it then because it scared me. This time I took note of it. I sat in my car outside the law office perfectly still, allowing myself to sit in the feelings that were rushing through me.

A long time ago I'd learned about something called the butterfly effect. It is an underlying facet of chaos theory. The butterfly effect says that an event in nature as simple as a butterfly flapping its wings can set off a series of events that can result in something as massive as a tsunami on the other side of the world. When I first heard of it, I thought, what great misfortune it would be to feel the softness and beauty of a butterfly flapping its wings against your skin and dismiss it, not knowing its potential devastation to your life or the lives around you. Those events might appear chaotic, random, or unconnected when, in fact, they were meant to be interconnected, leading to a particular outcome that you don't know about until you do. In that moment, sitting in my car, that unsettled feeling was the flutter of butterfly wings. I didn't know what to call it or where it was leading but I knew it was important. What I didn't understand was how it would change the trajectory of my whole life.

mercy, mercy me

There are few things more painful than watching the folks you love actively not love you back. Especially when they aren't outwardly unkind or distant or they've spoken words that sounded like love and have provided support that could be construed as love without an understanding of the kind of love you need and deserve. That is where I was with the Sanders family by the end of 2005. I had started to question them and myself for being so committed to them. In 2004, Hurricane Ivan hit Alabama while a boyfriend and I were on a weekend trip for my birthday. I was in the mountains of Tennessee and had left Kaia with Malika, Mrs. Sanders's daughter, my childhood friend and mother of my niece, Princess. When the family decided to leave Selma and find shelter away from the approaching storm, Malika called my best friend at the time, Annie, to come and take Kaia. My girlfriend was stunned and confused as to why they would leave Kaia behind in Selma while they left for safety. We were all supposed to be family. It was one of the first times that I started seeing the family dynamic a bit differently. The Sanders family were seen as leaders in Selma. They'd provided legal support, much of it pro bono, to Black people in the Black Belt long after the heyday of the movement. They were lead attorneys for the landmark Black farmers case, which led to a groundbreaking settlement. They had started legacy organizations like the National Voting Rights Museum and Institute, the Black Belt Arts and Cultural Center, and the 21st Century Youth Leadership Movement. Historians of the civil rights movement had written about the importance of their work. Their legacy is robust and important—I could never and would never take that from them. But I know in movement communities we have a habit of lionizing folks without calling them to account when they fall short. What is the point of a movement for liberation if we can't reflect the same dignity and accountability between each other that we are demanding from people outside of our communities? I was learning that the hard way by having my heart broken by people who claimed me as one of their own.

Their love was unsubstantiated by their actions, and it confused me because, in so many ways, I defined my worth by how much they and others loved me. Now, for the first time, I was feeling like it wasn't enough—like my heart was hungry for something else, but I didn't know what to look for because it was all I had ever had. I asked God to help me understand what I was experiencing, but prayer couldn't prepare me for the moment our family ties reached the breaking point.

〜〜〜

Reverend James Luther Bevel was a giant of the civil rights movement. He was one of Dr. King's chief strategists and lieutenants, and he was the architect of some of the boldest, most historic events of the movement, including the Birmingham Children's Crusade and the Selma to Montgomery March.

He was also a serial child molester.

Most of us had no idea about this when he began visiting Selma, eventually relocating there in 2004. I had first met Bevel as a camper in 21C, where he was a visiting presenter. He had a caramel complexion and was short in stature with a receding hairline that made a U-shape on top of his head and gray hairs on the side that connected to his mustache and beard. He was always dressed in some kind of pastoral clothing, but he was eccentric and vulgar unlike any pastor I had ever met, once telling the boys at camp that they needed to keep their dicks out of white pussy. As kids we found him odd but entertaining.

He arrived in Selma with a small army including his wife, Erica. She was exactly as Bevel seemed to like his women—light, bright, and damn near (or actually) white. She was also meek and malleable. He and Erica had a daughter who was about seven, the same age as Kaia and Princess. Others in his cult included an old guy who dressed like Bruce Leroy, carrying a machete and yelling at people; that man's grandson who was maybe thirteen; a group of women whose names all blended together to me; and his chief lieutenant, a man named Franklin. They were quickly invited into our community spaces and wasted no time showing us how disruptive and hostile they were. He and everyone he rolled with seemed smarmy and creepy. Every opportunity he got to hold court, he preached about his "philosophy of institutions," based on the six institutions that he claimed were laid out in the Lord's Prayer: church, government, business, home, school, and clinics. It was all bizarre, but that last one we would soon discover was the most important pillar, at least to Bevel.

Bevel's arrival in Selma coincided with a shift in my own life. I was growing increasingly aware of a hole in my work with the children at the Black Belt Arts & Cultural Center. The program was coed, but the boys tended to get more attention than the girls—negative and positive. It was second nature for us to assign the girls roles traditionally associated with domesticity, like cleaner and helper. We went overboard when it came to rewarding the boys for listening and following the basic guidelines of the program, but not the girls. It was a foregone conclusion that the girls would behave. I started taking stock of the number of girls who were having issues outside of the program—everything from academic struggles to being bullied to trouble at home—and how it impacted their participation in the program. At the time, I had a group of kids who were all from the same family. If there was something going down at the center, chances are one of the four girls—or the sole boy—was involved. Their families were from an area in Selma called the Viaducts because it was located by a series of small viaduct bridges. It was nicknamed "slave city" because the poorest residents lived in that area, on the outskirts of town, often without basic necessities like running water or indoor bathrooms.

The four girls—three sisters and their first cousin, Diamond—were some of the most beautiful children I had ever laid eyes on, particularly the oldest of the sisters. She was what old Black folks call "pretty Black," with smooth, silky-like skin, high cheekbones, perfect eyebrows, and a gorgeous, broad smile revealing pearly white teeth. Nothing but her circumstances kept her from a career as a high fashion model. Diamond was the ringleader, though. She was a particular kind of difficult, and she reveled in it. She specialized in pushing buttons and manipulating situations. No matter what she did, she would always come back at me with, "*What you gonna do, kick me out? So, I don't care—kick me out!*" I recognized it as a test and was determined not to fail. That one family kept me on my toes and as a result got a lot of special attention from me and the rest of the staff.

One particular afternoon at the Gathering Place, Diamond and her cousins got into a huge fight with some of the other kids. I stepped in with two other counselors, and we were immediately met with the girls' fists. When trying to fight grown-ass adults didn't work, the girls threw a long folding table at the plate-glass window at the front of the building. The table hit the glass with a heavy thud and fell to the ground. Luckily the window didn't shatter. The other two counselors and I stood there, stunned. I was determined to not give in to Diamond, but this was so egregious that I had to put my foot down. When we had the situation under control, I pulled her aside and told her that she would not be allowed back unless her mom came to talk to me.

The rest of the kids left for the day on the program van, but I stayed behind and waited for Diamond's mom. I'd called her after the altercation and left a voice mail, and Diamond had told her cousins in the program to let the family know that I was holding her here so they could "ride up on me" and get her out. We sat and sat and sat. An hour later, a passing car stopped in front of the center.

"Aye, you aight? What you doin' here?" someone yelled out. The vehicle belonged to Diamond's cousin, and the group of young men in the car were various other cousins and friends. I was tired and grateful that somebody finally showed up to pick up this baby.

Diamond called back to them to ask where her mom was. "Yo mama? Yo mama gone! She gone to Detroit I think she said." I watched this news land on Diamond like a bee sting. She went from stunned to furious.

"Nah uh!! My mama ain't go to no damn Detroit! Shut up! She coming by here because she fittna whup this lady ass for messing with me!" Yes, she was talking about me, and no, I was not phased at all. The boys pulled off and we kept sitting. Another hour passed and the van had returned from the nightly drop-offs. I decided I'd take her home myself. As we pulled up to her house, it was clear no one was home.

"Where do you go when your mama ain't home?"

"Round to my cousins," she said in a voice that paled in comparison to the screeching she was doing a few hours earlier.

"Where is that?"

Her chin was now planted in her chest, and she never raised her head, even though she raised her hand to point down the street. "Down Minter."

I drove her down the block and up Minter Street, no more than four minutes away from her house. She told me where to stop and when I did, I was staring out the window at a porch full of people, mostly men, playing cards and music and smoking and drinking.

"Who lives here?"

"My grandma and nem," she said. But as I looked on that porch, I definitely couldn't spot a grandma, but I did see a whole lot of "nem."

While I was asking her questions, a kid ran up to the van and started screaming, "Hey, African Dance Lady!!!" I didn't recognize him, but it made Diamond snap her head up and roll down the window to yell at the group.

"Y'all seen my mama?" she screamed over the music. No one responded and she asked me to beep the horn, which I did. That got the attention of one of the guys, who bounced over to the van. He had no shirt on, and he held a beer bottle in one hand while holding up his pants—a sign of respect—with the other. He got right up to the van and leaned his arm on the window, which allowed me to see his slits for eyes more clearly. It was obvious that he was high as a giraffe's pussy.

"Ayyyye lil mama, what's going on? You lookin' for your mama?" he asked Diamond.

The question seemed to give her brief hope that he knew where her mother was. She perked up. "Yeah, you seen't her?"

The young man licked his lips while looking directly at me and then turned to her and said, "Ya mama gone girl. She off to Detroit chasing some nigga. You know your mama."

And because this baby obviously knew her mama better than anyone, she knew it was true. She sank back into the seat and stared straight ahead for a moment before asking when her mother left. The man, who had greeted me at this point and told me that he was her cousin, replied, "Shit, I think this morning or something . . . I don't know. But she left Man over here. He in there."

Diamond was the middle child of three. She and her younger brother, Dougie were in my program. Man, who was about fourteen, was the oldest.

"You comin?" The cousin stepped back from the van. "You can come too, African Dance Lady . . . you gon' teach me some of that African shit?"

In the time it took him to climb those porch steps, I had made up my mind that I wasn't leaving her here.

"Diamond, I can't leave you here without talking to your grandma."

"Naw, she sleep. It's okay."

"You don't have to stay here. Can't I take you by your auntie's house?"

"Naw, too many folks over there already. That house small. I'll just stay here." Her voice betrayed her attempt to hide her disappointment, but I was running out of ideas. She opened the door and hopped out of the van. I hopped out on my side and asked her to come around. Now we were standing face to face. I said, "You don't have to stay here if you don't want to."

She looked me straight in the face and asked, "Why would I not want to?" She tried to mask her desperation with the last bit of attitude she could muster up. That tone tripped a wire in my brain. When I was a kid, I always wanted someone to *ask* me the right question. I could never bring myself to say it, but if I were just asked, I want to believe that I would have told. At the very least it would have felt like a beacon of light. Like there was someone *to* tell. All I ever wanted was to tell.

"Is someone here messing with you?"

She was built differently than her cousins, who had naturally slender physiques. Diamond still had a little baby fat but was starting to fill out in the way that so many Black girls do around her age. When I looked at her, I saw a squishy teddy bear with a round face and a button nose and heavy glasses obscuring her big, almond-shaped eyes. But I knew that others looked at her and saw a round behind resting on thick thighs that gave way to what the elder Black ladies called birthing hips.

She rocked back on her heels a bit before replying with great indignation, "No!" That told me all that I needed to know. I didn't respond, but I didn't avert my gaze. We stared at each other, her eyes roaming wildly back and forth and up and down, my eyes steeled directly on her.

"Is somebody messing with you?" I asked again.

This time she whispered. "No, ma'am."

"Okay," I said. "Well, let me ask you this. Do you want to go in this house?"

"No, ma'am," she whispered again.

"Get in the van."

My heart was racing. *What the hell are you doing, Tarana?* I was breaking the number-one youth worker rule in the book—don't do anything without express permission from a parent or guardian. But I couldn't find one, and this was urgent. I took a deep breath and got in the van after her. We fastened our seatbelts and I pulled off. When we got around to my house, I got out of the van. She didn't get out right away, so I called her name. As I started toward the back of the van, she finally appeared, and we ran into each other. I was caught up in apologizing for not seeing her when she reached out and hugged me—wrapping her arms around me in a vice grip. I could feel her body convulse as she started to cry a river of tears. I knew it was worth the risk I was taking, and I knew my work was about to change.

Diamond stayed with me for almost a week. Long enough for me to go to the store and pick her up some school clothes. Eventually her mother returned, and I took her home without being asked a single question as to why I had her. I still didn't have the resources I needed to help, but unlike all those years ago with Heaven, I was empowered to try.

My experience with Diamond only added to my disillusionment with the work of my elders in Selma. I needed to turn my focus to building a sense of self-worth in other Black girls like Heaven and Diamond. What I saw missing in

Diamond and her cousins and so many of these girls was a connection to how *valuable* their lives, current and future, were. Few things in their immediate surroundings indicated that it mattered if they lived or died, or if they were cherished or abused. As a result, they didn't talk about the abuse or the longing for death or any of the twists and turns between those two places that made their young lives infinitely more complicated. "What for?" and "Don't nobody care!" were repeated like mantras when someone would suggest they were worthy. I had spent many years feeling the same way about myself. Their resolve to bide their time until it ran out felt like someone flashing the glare of a mirror in my face. I didn't want to see myself, but there I was. And even when I closed my eyes to protect them from the glare, I could still feel its heat. I had to start thinking of myself as worthy if for no other reason than to not fail these babies—the way I had allowed myself to fail Heaven.

That same year, I started a program called Jendayi Aza with my friend Annie and another close friend. The program was centered around African teachings, based on the Nguzo Saba, or the seven principles of Kwanzaa and the principles of Maat. As we ventured into the space of girls' leadership, it became more and more obvious that our girls needed direct attention. Over the course of the next year, the program evolved into an organization called Just Be, Inc., which pulled from the two middle schools in Selma, C.H.A.T. Academy and an alternative school for all grades called the Phoenix School. Almost every girl between ages twelve and fourteen was exposed to what we called the JEWELS curriculum, which was built out of the original principles of Jendayi Aza. The program was not created to combat sexual violence but to build a sense of self-worth in Black girls by giving them tools to counteract the messages of worthlessness the world would inevitably push on them. I wanted them to know their history, to think deeply about the kind of contributions they wanted to make in their communities, and to create a road map for getting there instead of waiting for something magic to rescue them. But mostly, I wanted them to feel seen and heard and valued. In many of our sessions, which took place in school twice a week as a replacement for gym class, the girls did more talking than we did. It took a minute to get them used to having that kind of space after being told that they were too loud, too nosey, too talkative, or just *too much*, but once they opened up—they opened all the way up.

Between the Black Belt Arts & Cultural Center and Just Be, Inc., I had no time to engage with Bevel or his followers. They were bad news and I hated being around them. My daily schedule had shifted—I'd left the paper—and now I was at the museum every morning, four times a week for two hours. I was either at C.H.A.T or the Phoenix School in the afternoon, and then I did the after-school program at the Black Belt Arts & Cultural Center and was back at the museum to finish up any work in the evening. Bevel had been given blanket use of the museum facility and the Gathering Place next door. In an effort to revive a local chapter of 21C, Mrs. Sanders started a group called the Peace Warriors and recruited some local kids, which was her specialty, to join. Those young people were also sent to participate in sessions with Bevel weekly. A few of the kids overlapped with our after-school program, and I didn't like what I was hearing about these sessions so I decided to go see what was going on for myself.

Annie came with me and we made our way down the couple of blocks to where Bevel was holding court. We weren't in the doorway for more than a minute before we witnessed him forcefully pull a child to the front of the room and push a Bible into his hands. The boy was meek and his moves were delicate. He stood sheepishly in front of the rest of the kids. Bevel instructed the boy to balance the Bible on his outstretched forearms while reciting some bullshit that was written on a small chalkboard at the front. We couldn't make out the gibberish the boy was reciting, but Bevel began to scream about *faggots and fornication*! Annie and I were at a loss for words. We moved out of the doorway, unsure exactly what to do. We decided to relay what we saw to Hank Sanders. While Rose had set Bevel up with these kids, Hank—who was the only one who could rein in his wife—was more reasonable, we thought, and might be able to help.

Every time we went by the museum we saw Bevel saying something else inappropriate or obscene to these kids, and waited to see if Hank would take any action. After more than a few weeks nothing changed, and we couldn't stand aside any longer. One day I pulled our van up to the door, opened the sides, and went to the doorway of the Gathering Place. It was open, as it always was while Bevel preached to the kids. I waited until his back was turned and whispered to one of the kids to come to the door. She quietly made her way to the open doorway.

"Do you want to be here?" I asked. She shook her head no, and I motioned for her to go sit in the van. Bevel was turned away the whole time, but two of her girlfriends immediately caught on to what was happening and wanted to go too. Again, they waited until he was not focused on them and ran out and joined the first girl in the van. But they hadn't been as quiet, giggling as they ran out of the building. Bevel turned and shot daggers at me with his eyes. He flew into a rage, barking that we were disrupting his workshop, but it was too late to intimidate me.

Emboldened, I stepped through the door and announced to the kids, "You don't have to stay here. If you want to take dance or do crafts, come with me."

The kids sat motionless, and then one of them piped up. "Mrs. Sanders told us not to leave." Annie and I looked at each other in confusion.

"You don't have to listen to Mrs. Sanders," my friend said. It took only a few seconds to sink in before almost all the students got up and ran out to the van. Bevel didn't say a word, as if he wanted to see how it would all play out. We left him with maybe three kids, including the child he had humiliated days before with the Bible. I hollered for him to come too, but he said that he couldn't, and I didn't push it. The other kids were out, and we could always go back. I still had no idea the extent of his depravities, but I knew we had to get those children out, like we were headed North toward freedom.

unbound

Bevel's troublesome presence in Selma didn't stop the progression of our work. The middle school program was a huge success. We now also had a high school program and an after-school program, each with their own focus. The older girls were being taken through rites of passage in Jendayi Aza, designed to help them map out their lives in ways they could use over and over again as they moved forward in life. It was about interdependence and sisterhood and worth. The middle school girls were in the JEWELS program designed to make them think about the difference between who the world said they were and who they truly were. It helped them explore their relationships and figure out how they wanted to show up authentically in their own lives. The after-school program was about community action through arts and culture. Developing projects, dances, plays, and other forms of creative expression gave the young people a vehicle to contribute to their community where it was most needed. None of our work specifically addressed sexual abuse, assault, or exploitation, but among the three programs, we were dealing with it. We were dealing with two middle school girls who were gang-raped—one of whom tried to commit suicide as a result and another who got pregnant at fourteen and was made to keep the baby as punishment for "opening her legs." We were dealing with a girl who was in the Children's Home, the local foster care program, with the baby she'd had by her mom's boyfriend and pregnant with the child of another abuser. We were dealing with a girl who was sixteen and pregnant by a thirty-five-year-old married man. Her mother refused to press charges because "*Who gon' pay for that baby?*" And we were dealing with an administrator at the local high school who, we had come to find out, was allowing girls to get out of detention or other trouble if they went to his office and gave him a lap dance or, as in the case of the dance team member in our program, performed her dance routine privately for him while in uniform.

I was in danger of being consumed by my own feelings of inadequacy. Every story I heard and had no solution for rendered me stricken for days. Sexual violence was not part of our program but dealing with it was clearly vital to our work. What was the point of working to build a sense of self-worth for two days a week only to have it torn down the other five? We could do small things and we tried. My little muff, Celeste—who came up under me in 21C, was from New York and essentially like a little sister—caught a nineteen-year-old boy sexually assaulting a twelve-year-old girl in the bushes by a local park and beat the boy within an inch of his life only to then be arrested herself and have her attorney, Mrs. Sanders, convince her that she should negotiate to keep both her and the boy out of jail. I had to chase older boys and grown men away from our program and events—regularly. I took more girls like Diamond into my house when desperate times called for desperate measures, but it was not enough. It was imperfect, but it felt like the best we could do with limited resources and even less community support. Few people in our social justice circles saw this emerging work as real "movement" work. They classified it as social work—as if these weren't the same people who marched through streets chanting, *"Who will speak for the children? Who will call out their names?"*

The hypocrisy, the apathy, the sheer depth of it all was unbearable.

I walked into the museum one day to find Ms. Ann sitting in the window staring straight out, looking like she'd seen the devil himself. Kaia walked in first and was immediately directed to the children's room in the back. When Kaia was gone, Ms. Ann stood up, grabbed my hand, and pulled me down the long hallway past all the exhibits and into her small, private office. She still had not said a word, but she closed the door, went to her desk, picked up a folded letter, and handed it to me.

"Read it. All of it," she said.

I wanted to laugh at the dramatics, but something told me this wasn't the time.

"Ms. Ann, what is going on?"

"Read. It."

I unfolded the letter, which was addressed to Ms. Ann, and began to read

> *Dear Joanne Bland—We the children, family members, and mothers of some of the children of Rev. James Luther Bevel are writing to share information with you that we believe is urgent, and unfortunately, necessary.*

That first paragraph had my eyes opened as wide as saucers and my mouth agape. I shot Ms. Ann a look, almost not wanting to read on.

"READ," she said.

I looked back down and pressed on. I read about his "pedophilic activities" as described in the letter and the attempts to overlook and cover them up because of the importance of his contributions to the movement. I read about how he had a history of using religion, charisma, and manipulation to take advantage of and abuse the most vulnerable around him. I stopped reading after these few lines

> *. . . prominent members of the Selma community were involved for months, including a "community court" with Rev. Bevel and some of his children, in attempts to persuade him to acknowledge his conduct as a*

*pedophile over the last thirty years. At this community
court hearing, Reverend Bevel said that he did not
contest the accuracy of these charges including the
sexual molestation of four of his daughters . . .*

I felt heat rising up from my neck as the tears came
into my eyes. I stared at Ms. Ann in a mixture of disbelief
and despair.

She stepped forward, wrapped her arms around me,
and said, "I know . . . I know . . . Tarana, it's awful. And they
knew, Tarana. They knew."

Those last two words burned holes into my ears—
and my heart. They. Knew. The *they* being Hank and Rose
Sanders. The *they* being Malika Sanders. My friend. My sister. She knew. She knew and still she was dating Franklin,
Reverend Bevel's self-proclaimed "chief lieutenant" and
right-hand man, who had told us he had parted ways with
the cult leader because he disapproved of his relationship
with Malika. Reverend Bevel still had access to community
children, and where he didn't, his minions did. He breezed
in and out of the museum office freely and frequently—giving him access to my child as well. I was sick.

Ms. Ann and I pulled ourselves together and quickly
realized our new problem. What were we going to do about
it? As obvious as the answer may have seemed, it was not so
cut and dry. There were no protocols in place. We had never
faced anything like this head-on. When it comes to sexual
violence in the Black community, the culture of secrecy and
silence is more complex than just wanting to protect the
perpetrator. The long history of false accusations of sexual

violence against Black men along with our tumultuous relationship with law enforcement is a factor. The pain of watching folks twist themselves out of shape finding new ways to blame little Black girls for their own abuse plays a part. And the general ranking of sexual violence as minor in the face of things like structural racism and crippling poverty also play a role in how hard it is for us to stare down the monster that is sexual violence and call it out by name.

I believe that our legacy of living under the oppressive reach of white supremacy has trained us to take on shame that is not ours to carry. It's a training that tells us we must have done something wrong or played a role in causing this harm in some way, however small. Ms. Ann and I were ashamed that we didn't already know and that we hadn't already acted. We agreed Ms. Ann would go to Senator Sanders with the letter and her concerns. Since it was addressed to her, she thought it best not to disclose that I had read it as well.

Her meeting with the senator did not yield much, not even an apology. Instead, Senator Sanders asked if she had shared the letter with anyone else, and when she said no, he asked her not to. He assured her that measures were being taken. *That's it.* Nearly a year had passed between the time when Bevel's children had come to Selma to confront him a *second* time using the community court model and when that letter was written. The first confrontation, which happened months before the second, also in Selma, almost ended in violence between Bevel and some of his children. We saw less and less of Bevel after Ms. Ann went to Hank, but his tentacles had already spread around Selma, and the effects were showing up everywhere. The teenage grand-son of one of his followers sexually assaulted a six-year-old in our circle. One of his sons was accused by several teen-age girls of inappropriate sexual behavior. And worst of all, there was a trafficking ring involving the teenage girls in Peace Warriors, the youth program Rose had allowed Bevel to bring his teachings to.

Bevel had been given shelter by my elders, my mentors, my teachers—the very people I loved so unconditionally and who, I believed, loved me back. They didn't just carry his secret; they allowed him to be around the children they claimed to care for—community children, their children, my child. The betrayal was dizzying. My whole life, my response to harm had been to take what was coming to me, pack it neatly in a container, and put it away. Now, it wasn't just me who was harmed; it was those I cared about and felt respon-sible for. And even if I had work to do in understanding that I wasn't a receptacle for harm—I was certain that my child wasn't, and neither were the children in my community.

The shift from that day forward was swift but not easy. I knew it was possible to both love and loathe a person, but I had no idea what it did to the person carrying those two emotions simultaneously. One has to dominate, or they will cancel each other out and leave a shell where their host used to be. I tried to act normal, though we had strayed so far beyond normalcy that I was afraid I wouldn't be able to find my way back. Weeks and months passed, and the letter about Bevel didn't have as much of an effect as it should have, but it did strengthen my resolve to help the growing number of Just Be girls who disclosed their abuse.

I decided to reach out to the guidance counselor at C.H.A.T. and ask for help. Although she was well liked in the school and generally approved of our program, she and I didn't always see eye to eye. She once walked up on me while I was teaching a group of my girls how to slap-box and asked loudly, "How are you teaching these girls to be young ladies if you out here acting roguish with them?" I walked right up to her and said, "Sometimes slapping the taste out of someone's mouth is better than punching them in the throat. Don't you agree?"

I was only in her office now because I felt completely out of my depth. I wasn't trained as a counselor, I hadn't studied social work, and I didn't want to make a misstep that might cause more damage. After explaining what I had encountered, the counselor pushed back her chair and stood up to walk behind her desk to the long bookcase filled with giant binders. She took a minute to pull and push back several of these enormous notebooks until she came across a large white one. She lifted it up to blow away the dust that had collected at the top and then plunked it down on her desk. I sat in silence, knowing that whatever I needed to help my girls was not going to be in that binder. I listened as she ran through the school protocol for mandatory reporters, teachers and other school officials who are required by law to report any instances of abuse to the authorities. She paused momentarily to make sure I was a mandatory reporter, and when I couldn't confirm, she continued rambling on about best practices that I was sure she did not employ her damn self. I left there disheartened but still determined to figure this out.

After sharing my disappointment with one of my elders, Ms. Pat, she suggested I go visit the local rape crisis center. I hadn't even known Selma had a rape crisis center. I looked it up and it turns out they handled sexual and domestic violence. I found the address and drove over. I pulled into the parking lot of what looked more like a modest house than a center. Directly next door was a motel-like building with a long balcony positioned in front of a row of doors. Some men were sitting on folding chairs on the balcony. When I got out of the car, a few of them catcalled me. I ignored them, but I couldn't shake how awful it would feel to be greeted by this if I had recently been sexually assaulted. I walked up to the door, which was covered by an iron gate. It was locked. Everything about this felt odd. I thought maybe I had arrived too late, but it was thirty minutes before the listed closing time. I noticed a bell and rang it. Within two minutes a woman came to the door and opened it only wide enough to fit her body through the space. She was an older white woman with white hair, and she was holding a cordless phone slightly turned from her ear so that she could address me.

"Can I help you, sweetie," she said with that tone of voice that really meant, *What do you want?*

I was already put off, but I pressed on. "Hi, I work at the local junior high school, and I'm looking for some resources for the young girls in my program who—"

"Let me stop you, sweetie," she said. "We don't take walk-ins. If you have a *situation*, you need to go on down to the police station, file a report, and then we will either send someone to meet you there or they will give you a referral to come back here, okay?" She finished her rundown and began to move back inside to close the door. The word *situation* echoed in my brain, but I recovered quickly enough to stop her before she shut the door in my face.

"Umm, okay, but do you have some information I can maybe use for my kids? Some pamphlets or something?" I asked indignantly.

"Pamphlets," she repeated. "Let me see." She stepped back into the building long enough for me to take a quick glance around the space, which looked clinical and uninviting from what I could see. She returned with a handful of brochures, gave them to me, and bid me good night. I could not believe I couldn't find anyone to help me, especially among people supposedly trained to do so. I wanted to be angry, but the anger didn't come. Instead, there was something else rumbling deep within me. I walked back to my car, a distinct uneasiness in my gut, and as I got in and pulled the door closed, the feeling overwhelmed me. I rocked back and forth in the driver's seat, forgetting about the men watching from the balcony.

I began to scream and cry uncontrollably, pounding my fists against the steering wheel. I had brought girls into my home, I had stood up to my elder and mentor, and I had asked people for help who a year ago I would never have dreamed of asking. "No, God!" The anger and desperation finally broke through in my voice. "No! Please, no." I was pleading now. I had never let the rumbling come to the surface before, but it'd been there for a long time. I shut my eyes tight and let my hands fall to my lap, exhausted by the helplessness I felt in that moment. I asked God where all this left me. *What could I do now? How was I going to help these girls?*

A stillness came over me and the rumbling settled. I heard, or felt, an answer. *It's you.* I opened my eyes and looked around, but I already knew. I was so certain that it frightened me. I wanted to continue wailing like I didn't hear it, but I did and now I couldn't unhear it. *But why me?*

I had created what I thought was a formidable coping mechanism for all the ways my past experiences and present situations haunted me. I had compartmentalized my life and kept a huge open space to store the bad things—my own internal dusty attic. My attic held violence, death, disappointment, and all their cousins. I almost never opened that door—I barely walked down the hallway that led to it. The system had worked, or I'd convinced myself it did, but now it was unraveling, and it was taking me with it.

I had stopped spending time with the Sanders family, though they didn't know the extent to which our relationship had been ruined yet. Malika had since married Franklin, the former chief lieutenant, who had by now denounced Bevel and his teachings. Bevel's wife and several of his followers still had refuge in our community, but he was mostly gone, it seemed. I had stopped attending the Sanders's events, and I knew people were starting to notice. Every day, I wrestled with why I didn't make a bigger deal about the Bevel news. I had confronted Malika and Franklin, but they responded only with frustratingly well-crafted answers. Franklin, who had been the closest to Bevel, swore to me and Annie that he knew nothing of the incest or Bevel's history as a pedophile. I left it alone. That didn't mean it left *me* alone. Since I had read the letter, I had started having chronic headaches. My doctor attributed it to needing glasses. But there were other weird symptoms. I was having "spells." They first came on during Hurricane Katrina, but they had gotten steadily worse. The room would spin all of a sudden, or I'd be overcome with pins and needles and need steadying. My mental health was no better. The kids in the programs made me happy, doing the work made me happy, but we still had the same challenges around sexual assault, and figuring it out felt insurmountable. We had dealt with everything from colorism to healthy platonic relationships in our JEWELS program, and now it felt like time to step it up. In all my searching for answers, I had been wringing my hands, thinking about prevention and overlooking the obvious. If these girls were telling me their stories, or indicating that they had stories, the damage had already begun. Yes, prevention was necessary, but it was beyond my limited capacity. Healing wasn't. I decided to write down all the little things I had been doing to work on myself and all the bits of information that I had gathered in my short journey, and I started shaping them into a workshop.

I wrote out the story of Heaven. I wrote about how carrying my own shame had kept me from stepping out into the world to be who I was meant to be. And then I wrote about the celebrities who I knew the girls looked up to and whose stories of survival inspired me over the years, like Mary J. Blige, Fantasia, Queen Latifah, Gabrielle Union, Oprah, and of course, Maya Angelou. I wrote down a list of words that I wished someone had explained to me when I was their age. I defined things like *grooming, rape, incest, disclosure,* and *shame.* When I looked up it was dark outside. I had been writing—longhand—for hours. I felt good about what I had put down on paper, but it still felt incomplete. Parts of my own experience were embedded in what I was creating, but I knew I needed to share my actual story, something I never *ever* did. I didn't even know where to start. I put down my notepad and sat on the edge of my mattress with my legs folded over one another and my back curved in a deep *C*. I hung my head and said a quiet prayer, asking God to intervene and lend me support. And then I did the unthinkable. I remembered. All of it. On purpose.

I closed my eyes and saw my little brown face surrounded by the faux fur of my favorite blue winter coat as I walked up the hill toward Mr. Bright Eyes candy store. I saw my friends KK and Lamont with me in the store, looking in the candy case. I saw *him* come in and come over and speak to us. I don't know what he said. I don't know what made me leave with him. And then I saw myself walking down the hill holding his hand. I pulled myself out of the memory and reached for my water and the Bible next to the bed. It took a while, but I eventually made it through the entire memory. I took breaks, but I always returned. I imagined myself walking alongside little Tarana and the big devil watching my small face intently. I tried to read my mind. I tried to pinpoint the moment when I realized I was in danger. I saw myself come into my apartment scared of the consequences, and I listened to my scrambled seven-year-old brain trying to put the chaos of what she had just experienced in order. I walked with her to face my mom and Mr. Wes. And then I had to stop. I opened my eyes as they brimmed with tears and lay there trying to soothe myself.

You are okay, I told myself. I pinched my forearm. *You are alive. You can feel.* I tapped on my chest, trying to bring myself back from the burning bridge I felt I was walking toward. I lay there for a while. My eyes were heavy, but as I closed them, an image appeared, and then another one. I sat straight up in bed. "NO!" I shouted. Another image popped in and I shouted again more forcefully, "No, Tarana, NO! Stop." In my mind I was running at top speed down the hall to get to that attic door. I had made a mistake. This building was on fire, and I was about to be consumed by it. Another image came and I sobbed, knowing everything was about to come flooding out of that door. My heart was beating as fast as a playing card stuck between the blades of a box fan.

And then I heard Kaia's voice. "Mommy . . ."

I heard the unmistakable sound of footsteps slowly making their way across the long living room of our loft apartment. I threw my hands over my mouth and gripped it tightly to keep another scream from coming. And then I slid my hands down just enough to speak clearly.

"Go back to bed, baby. Mommy's okay. Don't come down here, okay?" I tried desperately to calm the trouble in my voice. My baby had a sixth sense for trouble.

"Are you crying?" Kaia asked gently in the darkness. The rumbling threatened to burst.

"No, Mommy doesn't feel good, baby. Go back to your room." I squinted into the dark, trying to make out how far Kaia was from me.

"I can get you some water, Mommy."

I knew my baby. Kaia was as much my caretaker as I was theirs. My heart was still racing, and I was barely able to hold the tears at bay. I needed to keep Kaia away from whatever was happening here. "No, thank you, baby. Good night," I said and waited. I could feel their intense contemplation in the stillness of the room. The floor creaked slightly. And then creaked again. "Goodnight, Mommy." And then the footsteps headed to the back of the house.

I flipped over on the bed and started praying with all of the fervor I could muster.

"Please God, don't do this. Please, please, please God, don't let them come!" I was praying in a loud whisper. I heard the faint sound of the toilet flushing in the back of the house, and I lay flat on my bed like I was hiding. I *was* hiding. From my baby, and my memories. My cheeks were slick, and I could feel the wetness sinking into the mattress. I was glued there by my sweat and tears. I was losing control, and the images poured into my consciousness. I saw, with haunting clarity, the dirty, fast girl. It was no longer little Tarana in her blue coat—the victim. The other Tarana had found her way out and was moving around me like a spirit. I wanted to physically wrestle her back, but to do that I would have to scream and cry and the baby—my baby— would know. I lay there, with my eyes wide open, watching my worst nightmares unfold. I wasn't screaming or wailing anymore. My throat felt like it was on fire as I silently mouthed my prayers. I begged God to help me or to stop this torture. I don't know how much time passed in this paralyzed state, but the sun had come up at some point. I was still glued there, now quietly moaning.

I heard the toilet flush again, and it snapped me out of it for a moment. I could move my arms and my phone was within reach. I called Annie, who had keys to my house, and asked her to please come get Kaia. She lived a block away and was at my house in minutes. From the mattress on the floor, I saw her feet as she came in the door. She went directly to Kaia's room, and then as fast as she had entered, the two of them scurried out, thankfully without saying a word to me. She later told me that it was the first time she'd heard that level of terror in my voice. She instinctively knew to just get the baby and go. When they left, I finally fell asleep.

It was dusk when I woke myself up screaming. My sheets were drenched in sweat. I could barely see, but my mind's eye still could, and when I tried to open my eyes, another horrible image appeared. This time I wasn't paralyzed. I threw my body across the bed and tossed and turned violently, screaming and screaming. I prayed, loudly. I reverted back to my Catholic childhood and started reciting the Hail Mary, the Our Father, and the Act of Contrition over and over. I was so thirsty. The water was gone, and I desperately needed more. I attempted to crawl off the mattress and could not. For the first time since this fit started, I felt like I was losing my mind. I began to crawl around in circles on the bed and ask God why he was doing this to me. I opened my Bible and read aloud. The story I turned to was of Ruth—the woman who vows to stay with her mother-in-law, Naomi, after her husband, Naomi's son, dies. In the Christian and Jewish faiths, she is heralded as a symbol of loyalty and devotion. I read it a few times and then flipped again. This time I landed on Psalm 139. I started to read it aloud, but I kept stopping at the first line: "You searched me o' Lord and You know me." I lulled myself back to sleep, reciting those words over and over again.

I woke in the morning. The sun streamed through my floor-to-ceiling windows, wrapping the entire room in its light. I lay for a moment with my eyes closed, basking in the light and letting the warmth of the sun caress my face. Slowly, I opened my eyes and looked around the room. I saw notes scribbled in my Bible and across the bed on ripped-out pieces of paper. The sheets were half off the bed and partially crumpled on the floor. When I tried to move, my body felt like I had been beaten and dragged. I carefully stood up and made my way to the bathroom. As I passed through the house, everything else looked like it had been suspended in time. I returned to my bed and sat still for a while trying to shake the dizziness.

My mind was still racing, this time not with sordid memories but with curiosity. I had so many questions. My brain was overflowing with them, but I wasn't scared. I pulled each one apart one at a time and laid them out. I was in a trance, so hyperfocused on analyzing the events of the past day and a half that as clarity came bursting through, I'd exclaim out loud, "Ooh," "Wow," or "Okay." The memories hadn't stopped; they just didn't frighten me anymore. The scary drumbeat had become a melody in my head, and it soothed me. And then I saw Heaven. It had been nearly a decade since that day in the hallway at summer leadership camp, and every time I thought about her, I broke down. How different would her life be if I had found a fraction of the courage that child had? How different would all of this be: Bevel, the Sanders, the girls? How different would it all be if I just had a little bit more courage? *But what was courage? I wondered. How could I find it if I didn't know what it looked like? Maybe Heaven had courage because she had me. Maybe community creates courage? What if courage creates community? Maybe empathy creates courage? How can you express empathy toward others if you can't empathize with your-self? Is the core of healing empathy and courage?* The questions were coming faster than the flashbacks now, but so were the answers. Not in my head but in my heart, which felt like it was going to burst wide open. For the first time in my life my story was completely out of my body and I had finally told it to the one person who needed to hear it most, myself.

I searched around for a blank piece of paper. I wanted to capture this while it was coming. I found a steno pad that hadn't been used and picked up a pen. I opened the pad and at the top of the page I wrote two words.

me too.

end of the road

I couldn't stay in Selma. So much had shifted in my body, my spirit, and my mind, and I knew it could not be contained in this toxic little town anymore. I loved so many of the people there, but there was nowhere left for me or my child to go, or grow. Friends and loved ones had been telling me that for a few years, but I had resisted it until now. I had been doing the personal work that would support all the other work, and now it was time to put it out in the universe.

I was in the middle of cooking dinner one night not long after the episode with the flashbacks when I got the intense feeling in my chest that we needed to leave. It didn't hurt and I wasn't alarmed, but I felt like I was being gripped. I pulled the food off the stove, turned off the eye, and told Kaia to get in the car. We drove to Walmart, but I didn't do my usual meandering through the electronics and women's clothing sections. Instead, I marched straight to the storage aisle. I loaded up my cart with as many dark gray bins as I could and went directly to the checkout line.

An employee offered to help me get the bins to my car when he saw me struggling to balance them all in my cart and keep track of Kaia at the same time. I did my best to guide him through the parking lot and around the steady stream of customers making their way into the store, but he was having a worse time than me steering the cart. He was trying to make small talk, which didn't help.

"Can I ask what you using all of these bins for, ma'am?" He was panting and trying to see beyond the gray plastic tower.

"To pack up my house," I replied, steadying the cart for him. We finally reached my car and I popped the trunk.

"Oh, that's why you got so many! You about wiped us out! You must be moving soon?" he asked.

"Don't know when," I said, trying to arrange the bins so as many as possible could fit in the trunk before I started filling the back seat.

"You don't know?" He was understandably confused. "You packing up before you even know when you movin'?"

"Yup," I said calmly, continuing to try to clear this Tetris board.

"Well, where are you moving to?" he asked, determined to keep this conversation going.

"Don't know," I said in the same tone.

He stopped pulling the bins out of the cart and stood back. "Aight, don't tell me then. It's fine." He laughed a little, which made me laugh.

"I don't know! I mean that. I'm not trying to *not* tell you. I would just say, 'None of your business' if that was the case."

"So, ma'am, pardon me for asking, but how are you buying all these bins and packing up your house and you don't know where you are going or when you're going there?" He was now staring at me dumbfounded, leaning on the back of my car with one hand and the other on his hip.

"You won't believe me if I told you," I said, but he was insistent.

"Ooh, no, ma'am. I have to know this, and I will believe whatever you tell me."

"Okay," I said, ready to challenge him. "God."

"You saying God told you?" I nodded. "I KNEW it! I knew you was fittna say that—I swear I did."

"How?" Now I was the curious one.

He stood up and moved about six inches from my face. He leaned his head down and, to my complete surprise, whispered, "Cuz you walk like you got an anointing on you."

An anointing. My elder, Ms. Pat, had told me that so many times that I almost heard her voice when that young man said it. I'd asked her what that meant, and she would always say that *He* would tell me in due time, which in turn, frustrated me. But in the past year, I'd begun to believe her more and more. I won't say I heard God speak to me, like a voice, but in that moment cooking dinner I knew more than anything else that it was time to move.

I made several more trips to Walmart, getting more bins and packing supplies over the next several months, still with no destination and no move date. Soon Kaia and I were living out of boxes, and I knew it was time to be proactive. I applied for a job in Philadelphia with a youth leadership and enrichment organization and got an offer after the second phone interview. I accepted even though we had never laid eyes on each other. I figured if they trusted it was a fit, so would I. I'd never thought twice about Philly before, but New York, Atlanta, California, and the other areas I was looking at all came up dry. Then there was this one job posting in Philly—and I got that job. Maybe it was a sign.

Two weeks out from the move, I still couldn't find an apartment. *God, this is all you*, I prayed. *I don't have a hand in this at all. I'm just doing my best to be obedient. If this is your will, you are going to have to come in and fill in these blanks. Period. Again. This is all you, Big Dog.*

Feeling satisfied that I was still on the right track, I booked a U-Haul. I had saved up a little from my income tax refund and paychecks, but I was counting on money that the museum owed me for a huge curatorial project I'd done in my final months in Selma. The only missing piece was to let Mrs. Sanders know that I was leaving. I'd spent very little time around her and her family over that last year. While most of my other community family and elders, like Ms. Ann, knew of my plans already, Mrs. Sanders had no idea.

I ran into her while tying up loose ends at the museum. My stomach was doing its best Dominique Dawes impression, flipping all over the place, as I approached her. "Mrs. Sanders, I need to tell you something."

She stepped closer to me as if I was going to tell her a secret and tilted her head with anticipation, making one of her signature locs with a cowrie shell fall across her forehead. My heart skipped a beat. As much as I was disgusted and deeply disappointed by her and her family's failures in the Bevel fiasco, I also desperately loved this woman. This woman who had nurtured me and poured everything into me for nearly twenty years. This woman who told me that I had power and that I was a leader when I didn't believe it. This woman who gave me the support to make me believe it. And this woman who was beautifully human and flawed, not unlike other adults in my life.

"I'm leaving, Mrs. Sanders," I said, lowering my voice so she almost couldn't hear me.

"Say what?"

"I'm leaving."

"What you mean *leaving*? Are you going up to New York to see your mom?" I couldn't tell if she was genuinely confused or not.

"No, I'm leaving Selma—like moving away."

It took less than ten seconds for it to fully sink in, and when it did she screamed. "No, Tawana!!" and shoved me so hard that I fell into the gate behind me. The sudden act of aggression surprised both of us. I didn't know what else to do but laugh.

"Okay, Mrs. Sanders, dang!" I chuckled. She was not laughing. There was a look on her face that I had seen quite a few times before. Her bottom lip trembled a bit, and her eyebrows furrowed, and her eyes glistened with the slightest hint of tears.

"Why . . . ?" She started and stopped herself. We both stood silently for a few beats. "Why are you leaving and why so suddenly?" Her normally raspy voice was soft now.

"It's not sudden actually. I have been thinking about it for over a year," I explained.

"A year!" The hint of vulnerability was gone as her face shifted to anger.

"Yes, a year or so."

"And you didn't say anything to me? You just gonna pick up and leave?" She was growing more agitated by the minute. "We are supposed to be family!" Her words felt like a cold slap in the face. I wanted to scream back, "*FAMILY? Would family leave my baby exposed to her attacker and further exposed to a known pedophile? Would family have me struggling and living hand to mouth with no health insurance?*" I had been holding all of this and so much more and it could have all spilled out right then, but the truth was I didn't want to fight her. I'd told her what I needed to tell her.

I stood quietly, waiting for her to speak again. "When are you leaving?"

"In two weeks."

"Two WEEKS!" she yelped. Then she sucked her teeth loudly, spun around, and stormed off muttering without saying another word to me.

I walked to the back office of the museum and ran down what had just happened to the folks inside. One of the women who worked in the museum put her hand on my shoulder when I finished. "You know what's coming, right?"

I did know what was coming. Mrs. Sanders could be notoriously vindictive. As one of her favorites, I had not often been on the receiving end, but I had seen and felt it enough to know that she could be both insanely generous and wickedly unforgiving.

I didn't have to wait long for the other shoe to drop.

A week before I was supposed to leave, I showed up to the museum to get my last check. It was for $5,000. When I walked in I knew there was a problem. Ms. Ann and the other women looked at me somberly.

"What?" I asked immediately.

One of the women just shook her head and walked over to the window to sit down.

Ms. Ann was the first to speak. "Rose wouldn't sign a check for your fee. She said you owed her three thousand dollars rent, and she was taking it out of your pay."

I felt like someone had taken a bat to my head, and I took a step back like I was trying to avoid the next swing. Really, I was searching for my next breath. "She can't do that. I need this money to move." The tears welled up. "Why is she like this? I didn't do anything to her. I just want to leave!" Now they were streaming down my face.

"I know, Tarana. It's not fair. She's not fair. The whole thing is wrong!" one of the other ladies offered.

"What rent do I owe her?" Now I was getting mad.

My friend Annie chimed in. "Remember that time when the museum lost funding and they had to stop paying us, and she sat us down and told us that since we lived in the same house, our expenses were less and they would pay us five hundred—total—a month?"

"Yes, of course I remember! That was the longest five months ever."

"Right, and remember how she told you that you didn't have to pay rent because you were living in her rental house?" she continued.

"Yes. She told me that she would waive my rent."

"Umm, hmm . . . well, now she is saying she didn't waive it. She just let you stop paying until you got back on your feet. She took your three thousand dollars for back rent." We stared at each other. Annie had a way of speaking volumes with her eyes. Right now, her eyes were saying, *I told you these people were evil and not your family. Fuck this shit, and these people, you out.*

Ms. Ann stepped forward. "I know this ain't what you expected and I'm sorry, *but* it turns out that we forgot about some money we owed you from something else you did, so here is your back pay!" She was grinning from ear to ear along with the rest of the museum staff as she handed me a $2,000 check.

"Y'ALL!! You can't do this!" I screamed, crying again.

One of the other sisters came up to me and put both hands on my shoulders. "*We* can and *we* did. You are bigger than this little place and bigger than these little problems. Now you go and do what you were meant to do."

I hugged each of them, took my checks, and walked out the door.

~\|/~

Before I left Selma, I lined up my new homie, Nate, in Philadelphia, who I had met through mutual friends, to help me with the unloading of the truck. I just needed to find a place, pass the credit check, and move in right away. I started my new job in a week.

The first apartment we saw had a graffitied swastika on the door. We didn't even stick around to reject it. The second place had been rented in the two days since I had last checked, and the third place was just bad. The last place was off a street called Aramingo, and it seemed far away from everything. I was desperate, though, so it had to work. The apartment was decent enough. It was small and clean but nothing I would have picked under normal circumstances. The neighborhood was white working class, which alarmed me a bit, but again, I had gone to high school with similar folks, so I knew I could navigate it. At the end of our visit, I said I would take it. The guy who showed the place confessed he was doing it for his friend who was out of the country. He told us that he was going to contact him about getting the process started, but it could take a while. On the phone I had been clear that I needed a place immediately, and he'd assured me that I could move in right away. I didn't know what to do.

I left dejected. I was even considering keeping the U-Haul to live out of for a few weeks. Annie, who drove with me across the country to help me make this move, and I went across the city to meet her godmother, who'd invited us to join her for dinner that evening. I told her about the day and how everything felt like maybe I shouldn't have come, when she interjected. "I live around the corner in a very nice complex, and I know they have space, you want me to call the landlady? I know her very, very well."

Annie and I looked at her and said yes at the same time. Within an hour we had finished our meal and headed over to the complex. A lovely older woman met us and led us into a two-story building with four apartments inside. She walked in first and cut on the lights. I walked in behind her and took one look at the hardwood floors and midcentury flavor and said, "I will take it!" It was perfect for Kaia and me. Two bedrooms and one bathroom. A nice-sized living room with a view in the front of the greenery in the middle of the complex. The train station to take me into downtown Philadelphia was in the back. Plus, it was cheap.

I was starting to feel like my plans were not derailed after all. I followed the landlady to the office and filled out all the paperwork. The next morning she called to say I was approved.

I hung up and laughed. "God, you be playing! You be PLAYIN'!! You cut it real close this time. Like *real* close. But thank you. Thank YOU! I won't let you down."

God tested me in Philly. I was itching to figure out how I was going to continue the work I had started with my girls in Selma. The two words written in my notebook led me to write out a vision for how work to support Black and Brown survivors of sexual abuse, assault, and exploitation could come together. I added that to the drafts of potential workshops on this topic I had been toying with and created a session for the JEWELS. That session grew into a traveling workshop when some local teachers and youth workers asked us to bring it to their community. Before long we had a national campaign because I had created a MySpace page for both Just Be, Inc. and the 'me too.' Movement before I left Selma, and it had triggered an outpouring of requests for support and inquiries about joining from survivors. I was still trying to figure out how we could do more to build the work up beyond sending out tool kits and resources across the country. I also needed to get settled and get Kaia settled in a completely new place and in a new life far away and far different than the one I had created for us in Selma. The work always found me, though, in all aspects of my life.

Every weekend Kaia and I would put on a movie, and Kaia could relax for a few hours while I attempted to retwist or style their loc'd hair. I often used this time to open up more intimate conversations, because our after-school talks were always focused on assignments and chores. I knew they were stressed from the move. We'd arrived right at the start of fifth grade, and my child, the quintessential free spirit, did not understand city life or the antagonism of the other students. The bullying started almost immediately. I was afraid that it was compounding with unresolved feelings from our time in Selma. We'd talked about the things that they experienced but didn't revisit it often enough for us to really process it. Too often I felt like I was trying to pry information out that I was convinced they were hiding. I couldn't be sure if this shift I was witnessing to people-pleasing, validation-seeking behavior was a result of the excessive bullying or if something else had happened, beyond the Jubilee incident, to cause the change. I worried constantly that I had missed something, and that worry kept me on edge. One Saturday afternoon while I was doing Kaia's hair, I felt a wave come over me. A couple of times a year I asked my baby the same question: *Has anybody ever messed with you?* This day I felt compelled to find a new way to ask.

Everything I knew about sexual abuse and assault at that time came from my own lived experience, the experiences of friends and loved ones, or the experiences shared with me by an adult or child in our community. In our 'me too' workshops, I always told the stories of famous women who had experienced sexual violence. I didn't use their names—just quotes from interviews they gave. After telling the story, I would put it in a category, for example, *What she just described was statutory rape*, or *What happened to her was sexual assault*, or *This experience is sexual abuse*. After sharing the stories and explaining the categories, I would reveal the names. When I shared a name like Gabrielle Union or Fantasia, it always caused a stir. And when I added Oprah Winfrey and Maya Angelou, it would cause a full-on ruckus. These girls couldn't believe that the Black women they adored and admired had dealt with the same things and gone on to be somebody important and celebrated. Afterward, I would say to the group that no one ever has to share their story, but if they saw themselves in any of these stories, they could write "me too" on a piece of paper with their name or contact information or nothing at all. Sometimes, simply getting that bit of information out of their body was all they needed and all that they were ready for and that was okay. Those workshops took at least two hours. They often ran over because of questions and one-on-ones and a need for connection after such a heavy topic. Not all of the participants were survivors of sexual violence, but they all left with a better understanding about how sexual violence impacted their lives and how building a deliberate community was essential for healing and change. I always ended by talking about community. From how they could access community support to the kind of community we were building in this movement to how that community doesn't have to be a large group of folks. Sometimes community is just two people I would explain—as long as there is trust, love, empathy, and compassion.

That day in the house with Kaia there were just two people. And I felt like I'd failed our two-person community by not being able to speak fully about what had happened in Selma. But the feeling that washed over my body and rested in my spine that day caused me to sit straight up. It whispered, *This isn't about you.* I thought about when I was twelve, walking on the street with my mom and grandmother, desperate for them to ask me that *one* question. If they had, though, would I have answered honestly? I immediately knew that I wouldn't have.

I stopped doing Kaia's hair, took a deep breath, and bent down close to their ear. "You know there is absolutely nothing that can separate you from my love," I whispered. Kaia jumped and turned to look at me with eyes racing back and forth. I held their sweet little face like I did often and planted a big kiss on their forehead. I said it again but this time with more emphasis and context. "I mean it, my baby, nothing. There is nothing you could do or say or think that could make me not love you. You can tell me anything—absolutely anything—and I will still love you and do everything in my power to help you. Okay?"

Kaia looked up at me with teary eyes and nodded to let me know that they understood but they didn't speak. I felt the intensity building up in my baby's small body, and I didn't want to let fear take hold of the moment. I didn't want to push hard either. So instead I leaned on the work I had been doing with children everywhere else but my home.

"Baby, you know, if there is something you want to say but don't know how to say it, you can do like I tell my girls to do and write it down."

"Okay," they finally said in a small voice.

I got up and went to my nightstand and pulled out a notepad and a pen and gave it to them. As soon as I did, Kaia got up and asked to be excused to their bedroom. It seemed like forever before the bedroom door opened and Kaia came out of the room chin to chest. They handed me a folded note without ever making eye contact. Everything stood still, including my breathing. I had been waiting for this moment for so many years, but I never thought about what would happen on the other side. I took the note from my baby and watched them scurry away. I said a quick prayer, *Lord, whatever is on this paper we will handle together. I will need your strength to stand in for my own. I am not strong enough for this.*

I opened the paper. It said IT WAS A BOY AT CAMP. HE MADE ME DO BAD STUFF WITH HIS BROTHER AND I DIDN'T WANT TO. I'M SORRY MOMMY.

I felt my heart fold inside of my chest. That last line fell on me like a sledgehammer. My baby was sorry. My child was apologizing to me. Because like me, they thought that they had broken a rule. They thought that they were the bad one. How could I have not seen this all along? I was so hell bent on preventing my child from having the same experience that when it happened, I had not created the space for them to *not* have the same experience. I called Kaia back into the room and sat them down next to me. They were still staring at the floor, and now tears started dropping into their lap.

"I'm sorry, Mommy," my baby cried, falling into my lap and now heavily sobbing. I just held them and cried.

"Baby, look at me. You didn't do anything wrong. Nothing is your fault. Nothing at all. You are not a bad child. You are not in any trouble. Do you understand?"

Kaia nodded slowly in agreement, still crying. I could tell they weren't convinced, but I wanted to give them space to get there on their own. They laid in my lap for a while, whimpering and crying while I played with their hair. After some time, Kaia sat up and began to tell me the story of what happened to them. They were five and at a 21C summer camp. They told me who was involved and all the details as I fought to suppress my anger. They apologized again for not telling me because they thought they would get in trouble. And then, I realized that I had not yet done my part. In all the time I had spent thinking about and developing 'me too,' I was always clear that it had to revolve around the power of empathy, but I didn't share my story in the workshops. I had been trying to get Kaia to tell me whether something had happened to them, but I had never shared what had happened to me.

"My baby, listen." I raised them up so that we were facing each other. "When I was a little girl, a similar thing happened to me. That's why when I tell you that you are not to blame I know what I am talking about."

Kaia looked up at me, wide eyed with disbelief. "Mommy, someone did that to you?"

"Yes, a long time ago when I was about the same age as you were." It took everything in me to keep my composure, but then Kaia threw their arms around me and I couldn't any more.

"I'm sorry, Mommy. I didn't know! Are you okay?"

I held them close and wiped my tears. "I am okay, my baby. And you will be too. That is what I want you to know."

for colored girls

Philadelphia turned out to be the boldest, scariest, and best decision I had ever made for myself and my baby. I never regretted a day of it. I found the freedom to not just hear my own voice but to trust it—even through the mistakes. I found the courage to leave old baggage behind. But more than anything, I was able to clarify and sharpen my vision. I wanted to change the way the world thought about sexual assault, abuse, and exploitation, so that we would stand against it the way we stood against every other social ill. And until we could eradicate it, I wanted to make sure that no little Black girl had to hold the tsunami in her chest that I lived with for so many years. If I didn't do anything else, I could at least do that.

I left Philly and moved back to New York after Kaia graduated high school in 2015. It was two more years before the hashtag #metoo went viral. The viral moment created a space for so many survivors that none of us had ever experienced. So many of the folks who came forward and told their stories or even just said "me too" never thought they could ever say those words, or words like them, out loud, let alone have them validated by others and entertain the possibility of accountability. It was unheard of. But no matter how many hashtags there were, how many galas I attended, or how many celebrities supported the cause, I always turned back to the community 'me too' came from. Sexual violence doesn't discriminate, but the response to it does. In some ways, it is the great equalizer—no demographic or group is exempt—but the reactions to different people telling their stories are far from equal. That is largely why my work has always centered Black and Brown folks—particularly women and girls. The response to our trauma and our truths is wildly different than the response to white women's.

After the hashtag went viral, it became clear to me that many Black women were not engaging in the same public celebration of feeling freed from their stories as white women were. I wished for Black women to come forward. With the exception of a handful of women like the celebrities I used in my early 'me too' workshops, few Black women in entertainment spoke publicly about their experiences with sexual violence. That didn't change when #metoo went viral. Black women didn't see themselves in the mainstream media every day, and now they didn't see themselves represented in the faces of those who were bravely sharing their stories. We didn't see many other faces either. There also wasn't an outpouring from Asian, Latinx, Indigenous, queer, or trans folks. And when I talked to people from these communities the sentiment was similar across the board. The stakes were higher for them.

Before Cicely Tyson passed away, she shared one of the most heart-wrenching stories I've heard with Gayle King. She told her of an attempted sexual assault at the hands of famed acting coach Paul Mann, who attacked her the day he met her. This was a man who had helped launch careers of the likes of Sidney Poitier, Harry Belafonte, and Ruby Dee, so his classes were a sure pathway to her dreams. Through tears, Ms. Tyson told Gayle that it was the first time she had cried about what happened to her since the day it happened. And she talked about returning to complete the classes because she refused to let that one man deter her from her dream. I cried listening to the story because I thought about the scores of women just like her who saw no choice but to "forge ahead" and continue to interact with the person who had harmed them. And then I thought about how sad it must have been for so many Black women and other women of color to watch as white women took a leap of faith and told their stories. The women in Hollywood had, of course, endured agonizing scrutiny and endless harassment for speaking out—but they did, indeed, speak out. Many of their counterparts couldn't take that same leap.

I spent a lot of years—particularly when I was introduced to survival and healing as ideas that required practice—trying to make sense of why I survived. When I was in Selma, I rationalized that it was so I could do the work that I was doing. I thought the same thing when I was in Philly. No matter how hard the work, no matter how meager the resources, no matter how tired or frustrated or burned out I was, I always returned to it, not just because I loved my kids and I loved supporting survivors but because I needed to make the things I endured mean something. I was trying to make more space in the movement for Black women to find validity, accountability, community, and value. Even after all the work I had done to get myself where I was, I still needed that support too. It was a driving force behind my choice to participate in the *Surviving R. Kelly* series. Several months after #metoo went viral, another hashtag, #muteRKelly—which predated the emergence of the #metoo hashtag—started picking up momentum thanks to the shift in climate around sexual violence. Once again Black women were laboring to do what was right for our community. In 2018, I was asked to participate in a Lifetime documentary helmed by veteran writer, filmmaker, cultural worker, and organizer dream hampton. I had already spoken out about, written about, and taken to social media ringing the alarm about R. Kelly and his predatory behavior toward Black girls for years. In 2013, the *Village Voice* published an extensive investigative piece about Kelly. In the article they detailed years and years of allegations, arrests, cover-ups, payoffs, and lawsuits that supported the assertion that he was indeed a serial sexual predator who targeted vulnerable

Black girls. The article made waves, but it seemed like only Black feminists were yelling and screaming about it. White people loved "Ignition" just as much—if not more—than the Black folks who couldn't seem to turn him off. Kelly never fell out of favor or was disgraced, despite making vulgar music that rubbed our noses in the gluttonous ways he could describe the sex we all knew he was having with girls. He was one of the most successful R&B singer-songwriter-producers of all time. Kelly still played sold-out shows, was a mainstay on the radio, and was invited to perform at award shows and music festivals across the globe.

Everything about R. Kelly's legacy of manipulation, abuse, exploitation, and brazenness harkened back to my experiences as a child and in communities like Selma, where I saw predators like him protected. Survivors were always silenced, or shamed, and the community seemed to value whatever modicum of honor or prestige the predator represented over the lives and livelihood of the Black girls in that community.

During the taping of my segment for the documentary, as I talked about the devastation of Kelly urinating in the mouth of a little girl on video, memories of my own abuse and my shame and confusion, at being ejaculated on and thinking it was urine, came flooding back. It made me question why I was even doing this to myself. But the answer was obvious. Black women and girls deserved this moment. After years of enduring in silence and being skipped over as that veil of silence slowly lifted, we deserved to have our stories centered and our pain prioritized for once. Our whole community needed to see this. Black men needed an opportunity to rise up in unison and say, "He is not representative of Black men, and we absolutely reject him and remain committed to the upliftment and empowerment and protection of Black women."

But that didn't happen. What happened instead was a constant wave of attacks from the Black community, mostly men. My entire life has been dedicated to working in, and for, my community. I shouldn't have been surprised by the reaction from my own folks, but I was. The attacks and harassment were hostile and violent. I knew that if my work was to continue to center Black and Brown folks that I would have to figure out how to have this "family conversation." The vitriol and attacks didn't change the fact that so many women had come forward against Kelly, just like they didn't change the fact that Black women have the second highest rate of sexual violence in this country. But even with these facts, I understood the pain and panic that arose when Black folks heard allegations leveled at Black men. There is no escaping America's painful history of weaponizing sexual violence as a tool against Black men. The Black community is all too familiar with the fact that we are socialized to respond to the vulnerability of white women in this country. Black folks had seen too many instances of white women's tears marking the end of Black men's lives in one way or another. But surely, I thought, our community could see the difference between a Black man being railroaded by the lies of white folks and Black women disclosing the harm they had experienced from our men?

I think in some ways the backlash was also resentment that a light was being shone on an issue that we have been trained to be silent about. Black people are always carrying a sense of responsibility for uplifting the good name of our people because we are so used to others reducing our humanity and worth. While we absolutely have to name and work to eradicate the violence that Black people, particularly women and femme-presenting folks, experience at the hands of white men—specifically law enforcement both in and out of incarceration—we also have to name and work toward solutions that will interrupt the violence we experience at the hands of our partners, pastors, uncles, cousins, classmates, teachers, coaches, and others. Black men don't have to be excoriated in that process, but they do have to be prepared to listen, understand, and in some instances embrace accountability for the harm they have caused or make space for Black women and femmes. And because we have all been raised and socialized in patriarchy, many Black women have to do the same thing. Nothing about my work or life is about *not* loving Black men. Indeed, I don't believe you can practice love and be in community with folks without an incorporation of accountability as an ethic and a practice.

It all makes me sad for my community. My work is met with the old familiar cruelties and deflection of accountability from men, Black men, and boys—my own people, who I love so deeply. I have been called some version of *ugly* since I was a teenager—and it's almost always by Black boys and men. It makes me think of what Carrie Fisher wrote in her memoir, *Wishful Drinking*, "Resentment is like drinking poison and waiting for the other person to die." The people who hurl these vicious insults want to break me. They want to hurt me, and that comes from a deep hurt inside of them, a place that has to run and hide whenever it hears about sexual violence. Maybe because of memories of their own behavior or memories of their own abuse. Either way, I know that we won't make a dent in what is actually happening in our community until we can find space for these tough conversations. I don't see a pathway to liberation or healing from the legacy of white supremacy without a politic of grace and collective responsibility. That requires that we care for each other. While the hashtag moment created space for everything from public dialogue to court cases and some semblance of accountability for scores of non-Black women, Black women and other folks of color were not allowed this same space.

I have always had a vision for creating safety and healing in the Black community. It needed space to be nurtured, developed, and implemented. The glare of Hollywood and social media won't provide a pathway for that to happen, only we, in our community, can forge that path, and so I stay and keep on trying. And I will continue trying. It is why I share my story, and why I share the story of how 'me too' came to be. For Heaven, and Diamond, and Kaia, and little Tarana, and all the little colored girls who don't have any other option but to live, learn, love, and try to thrive in the places where they were harmed.

Just as when the tears came in the parking lot of the rape crisis center in Selma, now my spirit knows I am called into this moment to do something more than represent a movement. It knows that this movement is more than a hashtag and bigger than any one individual.

If unkindness is indeed a serial killer, then my revelation is that I was my own murderer. I had taught myself to bend to my own unkindness first, so that I would be able to withstand the unkindness of others. I will not bend anymore.

The work of 'me too' and uplifting empathy in our communities is far from done. I—that little girl in the stairwell, that ugly girl in the drugstore, that dirty, used-up dishrag— am also the girl who read voraciously, the girl who turned from fighting other girls to fighting for freedom, the girl who became a woman and claimed her voice as a leader. I am the woman who organized and fought and taught, the woman who despite all odds and in the face of trauma, kept traveling until she found her healing and her worth.

I am her.

She is me.

And we are free.

epilogue

Some years ago, I went back to my old neighborhood for the annual Father's Day celebration. I rarely returned to the block after Mr. Wes died because there wasn't much left for me there. But my mom went back often, and she would return with a commemorative T-shirt that listed dads from the community who had passed away. Mr. Wes, or Big Wes, as a lot of fellas in the neighborhood called him, was always listed, and seeing his name year after year felt like a celebration of his life. This year I returned with my mother, uncle, and some cousins. My whole family was from Highbridge, so it was a family reunion of sorts. Any apprehension I had about attending went away as soon as we arrived and I started to run into childhood friends left and right. We were laughing and hugging and reminiscing. It felt good.

And then I saw him.

The young man who had raped me when I was seven years old was now an older man, and he was staring directly at me. He was wearing all white and had on a pair of wire-frame glasses. His family, including his mother, my mother's friend, had set up a table next to the area where some of my friends had set up. My feet turned to cement. I was paralyzed in that spot. I stood staring at him directly in the face like a scared child staring into the darkness, convinced that the boogeyman was there. But the longer I glared, the more I realized that he wasn't staring back at me—he was staring *past* me. He didn't even *recognize me*. This monster who haunted my nightmares and daydreams for so long, this child molester who almost sucked all the possibility out of my childhood, this predator had the nerve, the luxury of not even thinking about me. Of not seeing me. My body unlocked and my blood started to boil. I wanted to run up on him and punch him, hard, in his throat. I wanted to scream, "RUINER!!!!!!!!" and then beat him bloody. But I did none of those things. I felt an anxiety attack coming on and made my way, quickly, toward the exit. Halfway across the huge open space I ran into my mother. A few years earlier, I had finally told her about the first incident and who it involved. She saw the look on my face and immediately knew something was wrong.

"What's the matter?" she asked hurriedly.

"He's here, Mommy. He looked right at me and didn't even know me!" The tears were coming.

"Who?" she demanded, looking confused and wanting a place to point her vengeance.

"Ms. Dot's son. He's here. Over there by where we were." She looked down to the end of the park where we were set up, and then she looked back at me with a desperate look in her eyes. What could she do, really? She was past the age of fighting men in the street. And I'm sure, even though she believed me, that she wouldn't know how to confront a man for his three decades' old crimes. "Can we just go, Mommy?" I pleaded in a small voice.

"Yeah, come on. Let's just go." She left with me right then and there. We didn't tell anyone. We didn't make any announcements. We walked out to the street, hailed a taxi, and headed back to her house. In the cab she asked me if I was alright, and I told her that I was shook up.

"Maybe he just didn't recognize me because he hasn't seen me since I was a very little girl," I said.

"No, he didn't recognize you because you turned out to be a smart, beautiful, accomplished woman despite him trying to take that from you." I sat back in the seat and cried some more, this time to myself. It didn't matter anymore that he couldn't see me because for the first time in a long time I felt like my mother could. He had not won—I had.

acknowledgments

The words on these pages were the hardest I have ever conjured up at one time. As much as I knew that it was time for me to find a home for them outside of my head and heart, at times I thought the very words would consume me to the point that I wouldn't find my way outside of their beginning and end. That didn't happen by the grace of God and the immeasurable generosity, kindness, patience, brilliance, understanding, input, honesty, and love of my village.

It is hard to put into words the depth of gratitude I have for the folks that walked me through this process—directly and indirectly. I am nothing if not thankful for each of you.

Mommy, I wish I could find new ways to tell you how much I love and appreciate you. You were my first teacher, and the lessons you seeded have taken root and helped feed the world.

Kaia, my whole heart in human form, thank you first for choosing me. Thank you for your continuous love and trust. You make me a better everything, and I am so grateful for you. Thank you for being patient with your mama and for lending me to the world yet again.

There would be no way for me to conjure these words and deliver them to the world without my day-to-day support system through this process. **Gerrick Kennedy**, my book doula, I can't say enough about your loving guidance and commitment to excellence. You pushed me and pulled me (and sometimes even shoved me!). We made it, and I somehow love you more! **Imani Perry**, aka The Wolf, you put the "Bam!" in Alabama, homie! You are "clutch" in human form and a low-key superhero—but your secret is safe with me! I owe you a debt of gratitude. Please know that I pay back in love. **Mervyn Mercano** and **Yaba Blay**, thank you both for thinking that you are the bosses of me—and then being that. Thank you for always showing up again and again. This book wouldn't exist without my four horsemen. I love you all.

Dani Ayers, **Denise Beek**, **Khadijah Austin**, and the whole 'me too.' International team. Thank you for allowing me to disappear into this process. Thank you for helping to carry my dreams and vision into fruition and for being so deeply committed to this work. I can't appreciate you enough.

To my sisters, the Aunties: **Vernetta**, **Whitney**, **LaTosha, Cookey, Camika, Maori, Jo-Ann, Radha, Elissa, Nzingha, Tamika, Akiba, April, Aliya, Kirsten, Shantrelle, Bassey, Biany, Dani, Denise,** and **Chancee**.

. . . and the Uncles: **Marc, Nate, Chris, Cliff, Babafemi, Marwan,** and **Doc**.

You all are so important to me—my chosen family. I love you and can't thank you enough for everything you have been to me—all of it.

There is no way to get through a life like mine without enormous support. So much of my support is not named in this book, but I want to give a special, heartfelt thank you to three: **Joanne Bland** (**Ms. Ann**), **Celeste** (**my lil' muff**), **and Annie** (**IYKYK**). You all have seen me through some of the worst and best parts of my life. But more importantly, this work could not have come to fruition without your drive, commitment, and love. I'm forever changed and forever grateful.

Chevarra Orrin and **Bacardi Jackson**. You are two of the most generous spirits I have ever met. Thank you for your patience and generosity. In many ways our stories are interwoven; thank you for trusting me with a part of yourselves. I hope I have been a good steward.

Fatima Goss Graves, **Ai-Jen Poo**, **Monica Ramirez**, and **Joanne Smith**—so many folks have walked me through these last four years but none with more patience, love, grace, and commitment than you four. I just want to thank you for everything.

Luvvie, **Denene**, **Demetria**, **Karen**, **Patrice**, **Kelly**, **Marie**, **Erika**, **Tayari**, **Stacey**, **Bassey**, **Britni**, **Shay**, **Heather**, **Samantha**, **Aliya**, **Kirsten**, **Carolyn**, **Tamara**, and **Deesha**. You all lifted me. Full stop. Love you OGs.

Kiese, I love and appreciate you, man. You make it less lonely out here on the ledge.

Glennon, your wit and wisdom are irreplaceable. Thanks for keeping a mainline open for me.

Prentis and **Shari**, thank you for helping me birth a new vision for and version of myself.

Brené (**Breneezy**), friend, you helped me turn this ship around. I am forever indebted to you for that and a good list more. Thank you for sharing your wisdom and opening your heart. And thank you for your steadfast belief in me.

Jennifer Walsh and **Dorian Karchmar**, thank you. From start to finish you both made me feel like the impossible was possible. Thank you for the encouragement and fierce representation.

Bryn Clark, you are a trooper. You met me as a colt and were determined to make a thoroughbred. Thank you for betting on me again and again.

To the rest of the team at **Flatiron Books**—**Nancy, Marlena,** and the many others that helped bring this book into the world, thank you.

To **Ms. Winfrey,** thank you for your "yes," and thank you for your courage and vision. It is unparalleled.

To my family, you all keep me going, but in particular over this last year **Malcolm, Tyrell, Latisha, Justine, Xavier, Nekia, Aunt Cecelia,** and **Uncle Neal**—you all have helped keep me sane and focused. I love y'all.

Granddaddy, you are the prototype. I can't imagine any other life but the one you handcrafted for me. I am forever grateful to be a Burke. I am forever grateful to be your child.

Grandma, I hope I make you proud. I will never suffer fools or take tea for the fever. You taught me well.

To **Taylar Bear,** thank you for understanding the long days and late nights. Thank you for your sweet check-ins and warm hugs and smiles. They got me through many nights.

Fatima, thank you for the warm embrace. I am so delighted to have you as a bonus baby. All in together, girls!

To my husband, **Sincere**, thank you for wrapping me in love everyday. You make me feel wanted and worthy and well cared for. Your sandwiches and random check-ins and pop-up hugs were like fuel for me. Thank you for being a sounding board and a silent partner when I needed it. From Bxdale to Bmore . . . it's always been you, baby. I love you.

So many people are responsible for making this book a reality, and so many people have played a role in making my life a reality. I know I missed names, but please accept my gratitude for however you contributed. I hope to have a long life with multiple versions of myself, but I will never run out of things to be as long as I'm grateful.

For you Tarana, so that you finally know freedom.